How to Manage your
Postgraduate Course

Palgrave Study Guides

A Handbook of Writing for Engineers   *Joan van Emden*
Authoring a PhD   *Patrick Dunleavy*
Career Skills   *David Littleford, John Halstead and Charles Mulraine*
e-Learning Skills   *Alan Clarke*
Effective Communication for Arts and Humanities Students
   Joan van Emden and Lucinda Becker
Effective Communication for Science and Technology   *Joan van Emden*
The Foundations of Research   *Jonathan Grix*
The Good Supervisor   *Gina Wisker*
How to Manage your Arts, Humanities and Social Science Degree   *Lucinda Becker*
How to Manage your Distance and Open Learning Course   *Lucinda Becker*
How to Manage your Postgraduate Course   *Lucinda Becker*
How to Manage your Science and Technology Degree   *Lucinda Becker and David Price*
How to Study Foreign Languages   *Marilyn Lewis*
How to Write Better Essays   *Bryan Greetham*
Making Sense of Statistics   *Michael Wood*
The Mature Student's Guide to Writing   *Jean Rose*
The Postgraduate Research Handbook   *Gina Wisker*
Professional Writing   *Sky Marsen*
Research Using IT   *Hilary Coombes*
Skills for Success   *Stella Cottrell*
Presentation Skills for Students   *Joan van Emden and Lucinda Becker*
The Student's Guide to Writing   *John Peck and Martin Coyle*
The Study Skills Handbook (second edition)   *Stella Cottrell*
Study Skills for Speakers of English as a Second Language
   Marilyn Lewis and Hayo Reinders
Studying the Built Environment   *Marion Temple*
Studying Economics   *Brian Atkinson and Susan Johns*
Studying History (second edition)   *Jeremy Black and Donald M. MacRaild*
Studying Mathematics and its Applications   *Peter Kahn*
Studying Modern Drama (second edition)   *Kenneth Pickering*
Studying Physics   *David Sands*
Studying Psychology   *Andrew Stevenson*
Teaching Study Skills and Supporting Learning   *Stella Cottrell*
Work Placements – A Survival Guide for Students   *Christine Fanthome*

How to Manage your Postgraduate Course

Lucinda Becker

First published 2004 by
PALGRAVE MACMILLAN
Houndmills, Basingstoke, Hampshire RG21 6XS and
175 Fifth Avenue, New York, N.Y. 10010
Companies and representatives throughout the world

PALGRAVE MACMILLAN is the global academic imprint of the Palgrave Macmillan division of St. Martin's Press, LLC and of Palgrave Macmillan Ltd. Macmillan® is a registered trademark in the United States, United Kingdom and other countries. Palgrave is a registered trademark in the European Union and other countries.

ISBN 1–4039–1656–X

This book is printed on paper suitable for recycling and made from fully managed and sustained forest sources.

A catalogue record for this book is available from the British Library.

10   9   8   7   6   5   4   3   2   1
13   12   11   10   09   08   07   06   05   04

Printed in China

Contents

Acknowledgements   vii

1 Introduction   1

The purpose of this book   1
Taking an overview of your course   3

2 Choosing and Beginning your Postgraduate Course   8

Becoming a postgraduate student   9
Assessment   15

3 Studying Opportunities   24

Seminars   25
Lectures   27
Visiting speakers   28
Conferences   30
Discussion groups   32
Tutorials   33
E-learning   34
Placements   36
Work-based projects   38

4 Your Skills Base   40

Your range of skills   41
Postgraduate skills development   42
Reading productively   42
Articulating your ideas   47
Reporting your results in writing   50
Writing persuasively   51
Presenting your work orally   53
Problem-solving   54
Thinking creatively   55
Planning effectively   58
Analysing and developing your skills base   59

5 Working with your Supervisor   64

How to begin   65
What you can expect from your supervisor   68
Developing your relationship   73
Life from your supervisor's point of view   77

6 Managing your Course   81

Taking control   82
Making connections   86
Keeping on track   89
Time management   92

7 What if Things go Wrong?   99

8 Teamwork and Networking   117

Analysing a team   118
Identifying your teams   123

9 Presenting your Ideas   132

Research presentations   133
Seminar presentations   137
Conference papers   140
Publication   143

10 Writing up your Research   148

Timing   149
Planning   152
Word count   159
Draft and rewrites   162
Creating a bibliography   163
Style   165

11 Moving on from your Postgraduate Course   170

Focusing on the future   170
Breaking into the career market   173
Creating a CV   177
An academic career   181
Achieving success   185

Index   186

Acknowledgements

I would like to thank Paul McColm for making this book so much more effective than it would otherwise have been. I would also like to thank Kate Howlett, who worked so hard to widen the book's appeal. I am grateful to Michael C. Milam for giving me so much support from across the Atlantic and, as always, Felicity and Anastasia Becker made light work of proofreading and ensured that the index is as comprehensive and accurate as possible.

1 Introduction

A postgraduate course is more than simply a period of study and research; it is also, crucially, a time for reflection and self-development. One of the greatest challenges that you now face is that of self-management, not only in your academic work but also in the ways in which you use the opportunities open to you to develop transferable skills that will be of benefit to you in all aspects of your future career. As a postgraduate, you are embarking on a journey that will be exciting, satisfying and challenging. You will spend much of your time feeling in control and focused on your course, but there will be stages on your journey when you might feel less sure of yourself and your studying, when the path ahead is unclear. That is where this book comes in: it will guide you through the rockier patches and help you to overcome any problems as you encounter them.

▶ The purpose of this book

This is not a traditional study skills guide. It will help you when you come to produce an assessed piece of work, give a presentation or face a seminar, but it is also concerned with the overall management of your course. Making a success of your time as a postgraduate involves so much more than just getting through the course. With this in mind, this book will give you guidance on the day-to-day processes of your course, but it will also offer you the opportunity to rise above the everyday aspects in order to take an overview, to take control of the experience of being a postgraduate. In this way you can make the most of this chance to develop your skills base, maximise your learning opportunities and widen your understanding, both of yourself and the subject area with which you are engaged. When you feel that things are going well, it will help you to assess your success and analyse where to go next in order to build on that success. When you feel isolated, confused or just plain demoralised, it will reaffirm for you that your difficulties are both a normal part of the postgraduate experience and entirely surmountable.

A guide such as this can be used in several ways. You will probably make an initial reading of the book and then refer back to sections of it as your course progresses and your needs alter. In order to make the support it offers as accessible and relevant to you as possible, each chapter begins with a troubleshooting guide which outlines the issues discussed in that chapter, helping you to get to the information that you need as quickly as possible. Each chapter closes with a spot guide, outlining the key points covered in the chapter, so that you can confirm your earlier reading and check that you are still on track. Throughout the book the emphasis is upon practical help and support, with examples to support the advice offered and effective techniques outlined in step-by-step guides to success in every area of your course.

Your needs as a postgraduate will vary according to your experience, existing skills base and expectations. There are three principal routes into a postgraduate course:

1. *The undergraduate route:* if you have moved straight from an under-graduate to a postgraduate course, you will be familiar with many of the demands placed upon you. Being asked to produce essays or presentations may not faze you, but you may need more help than you had anticipated in making the transition from being an undergraduate to a postgraduate. You will, of course, have expected the level of studying to be higher, but you might encounter other changes for which you are less prepared, such as smaller seminar groups, independent research, the relationship with your supervisor and the need to move towards a career beyond your present course. These changes are all part of the excitement of being a postgraduate, but you need to be ready to meet them as they arise and cope with every situation with as much confidence and energy as possible. If you have moved into the UK university system from an undergraduate course in another country, the challenges need not necessarily be any greater. You will, after all, be ready to face a whole new cultural and educational experience, and this book will help you to get your bearings in the early days of your course and support you as the course develops so that you can make the most of everything that it offers.

2. *Professional development:* a postgraduate course that is entered into as part of a plan of professional development can seem relatively simple in prospect. You are in command of your subject, you have experience in the field and all you have to do now is gain the qualification. The reality of a postgraduate course can come as a shock, as you face a way of working that may well be alien to you and become part of an academic community with which you are unfamiliar. You have all the tools that you

need for success to hand, of course, but you might need help in assessing those tools and then employing them to greatest effect as you work through your course. Postgraduates who see their course as merely part of their professional life can miss one of the most rewarding aspects of the postgraduate experience: that of moving away from your everyday work life to immerse yourself in a new way of working and a more considered way of seeing things, leaving you with a new view of both your work life and your personal and professional development. This guide will ensure that you can gain this new and revealing perspective.

3. *Assessment of prior learning:* it may be that you have become a postgraduate without ever having been a graduate, or perhaps your postgraduate course has little to do with your degree subject. In either case, the assessment of prior learning, or prior experience, is increasingly being recognised as an important route into postgraduate work. You may not have studied in a formal way for some time; in which case you will find this book useful both in helping you to transfer your existing skills into the postgraduate format and in reassuring you that you are not alone in your experiences.

▶ Taking an overview of your course

Whatever your route into your course, you are now a postgraduate like any other, with your own misgivings, perhaps, but also with a unique set of skills and experiences. One of the key aims of this book is to help you to recognise, assess and then develop those skills, both whilst you study and beyond your current course. However you began on this journey, one thing remains constant for the vast majority of postgraduates: time simply goes by too fast. You begin by thinking that you have plenty of time to achieve all that you have set out to do, and at points you might begin to feel as if you are on a never-ending course, but for the majority of the time, and certainly as you near the end of your course, you will be amazed at how fast it has gone, how quickly the experience seems to be over. It is for this reason that managing your course, rather than just getting through it, is vital. If you waste valuable time trying to work out where to be and what to do, spend anxious weeks worrying about how to get useful feedback or wondering whether you will be able to cope with the next task, you will never be able to regain that time – time that you need to be spending elsewhere. It is possible to get so much more out of a postgraduate course than simply a qualification. This is your opportunity (perhaps your only opportunity for several more years) to assess your abilities in a structured environment, meet new challenges that will hone your skills and explore subject areas and ways of expressing yourself that you may never have thought about before.

All this is possible, but only if you take control of the situation now and then move forward with confidence in what you are doing and an awareness of what you might yet do. Postgraduate courses vary enormously in what they have to offer and the ways in which they progress their students through a course. If you recognise the type of course that you are on, and consider other courses that might be available to you in the future, you will have begun to take control. Outlined below are some of the principal course structures, with a brief evaluation of their strengths and weaknesses from the students' point of view.

Taught courses

These courses are most commonly found in the early stages of a postgraduate career: masters courses, postgraduate diplomas or postgraduate certificates, for example. You are likely to find that the structure of the work is similar in many ways to undergraduate work. You will be asked to produce written pieces of work, perhaps to give presentations and complete more complex pieces of assessed coursework. Added to this, particularly if you are on a masters course, you will be asked to produce a piece of independent research-based work. This could take the form of an extended project or dissertation, which will vary in length depending upon the course that you are undertaking.

The *advantage* of this type of course is that you can rely upon the course tutors to guide you effectively through the process. You will be offered close supervision of any work that you undertake and your endeavours will be fully backed up by taught sessions. One of the key benefits, particularly if you have been away from study for a time or struggle to work in isolation, is that you are likely to find yourself working in a cohesive group of students, from whom you can gain support and reassurance.

The *potential disadvantage* of this type of course is that you may find yourself restricted in the work that you do. Although some independent research will be possible, indeed it is likely to be expected of you, you will essentially be following a cohesive and probably well-established course, which can curtail your freedom to roam more widely in your subject area.

Remember, if you are on this type of course, to make the most of the support that is to be gained from being taught directly in this way, but also make sure that you know as early as possible just how much freedom you will be given to pursue your own specialist area of interest as the course develops.

Research courses

Although doctorates form the bulk of research-only postgraduate courses, there is growing recognition of the value of allowing postgraduate students at all levels to tailor their course, and their research, to their interests and experience. This is particularly true in cases where professionals are aiming to gain a postgraduate qualification in order to consolidate and validate their career-based expertise.

The *advantage* of these courses is that they can fit in with the other demands on your time. They allow you the freedom to investigate areas of research that are of interest to you and can be spread over a greater period of time than taught courses.

The *potential disadvantage* of these courses is that they can leave you feeling isolated. You might be working for the majority of your time with one supervisor whose aim will be to support and guide you through your research. Despite the fact that your supervisor will be an expert in your field and will want to help you as much as possible, you might miss out on opportunities in your area of study unless you keep your ear close to the ground and ensure that you avoid too high a level of isolation.

Remember, if you are on this type of course, that you will need to establish a stable and wide-ranging support structure for yourself and ensure that you have a clear view of where your research might lead you in the future.

Combined courses

These are perhaps the most common type of postgraduate course. Even in the case of PhD courses there may be an element of teaching, particularly in the early stages, whilst those courses that are intended to be heavily based upon teaching may still have elements of independent research. It may be, for example, that a series of seminars or lectures form the backbone of a course, but that students are encouraged to follow their own line of study, potentially making such seminars and lectures appear to be optional.

The *advantage* of a course such as this is that you can have the best of both worlds, in that you can be supported by a taught course whilst being given the freedom to explore your own interests.

The *potential disadvantages* of this type of course are that you might find the structured part of the course onerous at times, or you might feel stranded if the research element is a final addition to the course, undertaken once the teaching has finished.

Remember, if you are on this type of course, that you will need to manage your studying to make the most of the taught element of the course by keeping one eye on how you can use it to support your research.

Distance and open learning courses

Increasingly popular, particularly for those courses predominantly aimed at postgraduates who are juggling other commitments with their studying, these can be an attractive option. They are likely to rely upon a combination of teaching formats, from the Internet and emailing, to hard copy teaching packs, to occasional contact backed up by individual tuition.

The *advantages* of courses such as these are clear: you can fit your studying around your professional and personal commitments, you can work to some extent at your own pace and you can learn within a medium that suits you (particularly if you are technologically minded).

The *potential disadvantage* of this type of course is that it might not be as flexible as you had assumed. There may be rigidly imposed time limits on the production of work, or it might be that occasional direct contact teaching sessions (evening sessions or Saturday schools, for example) are a compulsory part of the course and yet do not fit into your work pattern easily. You might also feel isolated, aware that there are many other students on the course, but finding the contact that you have with them (perhaps via Internet study chat rooms) inadequate in making you feel that you are really part of a cohesive student group.

Remember, if you are on a course such as this, to make sure that you impose your own structure on your working patterns as early as possible and try to grasp all the support offered to you during the course, even if it takes some effort to find and make use of it.

Work-based courses
If your postgraduate course is intrinsically bound up with your professional life (for example a postgraduate qualification in a vocational subject), most of your studying may be a formalisation of your professional experience. You will be guided by your tutors and supervisor, but you might also be relying heavily on colleagues to support your work.

The *advantage* of this type of course is that you will feel as if you are gaining a recognised qualification as you go through your normal working life. You will be analysing and validating what you are already doing, which can make the transition into studying easier.

The *potential disadvantage* of this type of course is that your colleagues may be less understanding about the demands of the course than you had hoped, particularly if they have not undergone a similar course. You might also find it frustrating to be working on an academic level, yet not to be given the time to simply sit and contemplate the wider implications of what you are doing.

Remember, if you are on this type of course, you will need to ensure, well in advance if possible, that everyone whose help you will need is aware of exactly what the course entails, how much time you will need to complete it satisfactorily and the level of support that you may need.

As you can see, each type of course brings with it both advantages and potential disadvantages. In reality, many courses combine all the elements mentioned here, and you will work your way through the challenges of each whilst ensuring that you get the full benefit of every opportunity to advance. You will find that once you have understood and mastered the framework within which you are working, aspects of your course that once seemed confusing become much clearer. You will not be losing time worrying about the structure of your course and how that structure might impact upon your learning; instead you can get on with the tasks ahead of you with more confidence. Although it can seem daunting, it is possible to make the most of each element of your postgraduate course and so gain the advantages without losing out to any of the disadvantages. All that is required to begin this process is a determination to manage your postgraduate course, rather than simply letting it happen, and an awareness of what is involved and what is on offer. For you, reading this book is the first stage in that process.

2 Choosing and Beginning your Postgraduate Course

Troubleshooting guide

Read this chapter for help in the following areas:

- if you are thinking about applying for a course
- if you are trying to decide between courses
- if you want to check that you have chosen the right course for you
- if you are concerned that you might be underqualified to apply for a course
- if you are wondering where your course might lead
- if you are not sure about course accreditation
- if you are thinking about where to go after your course
- if you have not yet thought about specific learning outcomes
- if you need a course with a high level of flexibility
- if you are not sure how to find out about course options
- if you want to do more research on possible courses for you
- if you have not applied for funding
- if you have not thought about the differences between a new and established course
- if you are wondering how to choose a supervisor for your research
- if you are unclear about different forms of assessment
- if you are anxious about examinations

By the time you read this book you will probably have begun your postgraduate course, but it is still worth spending a little time considering all aspects of gaining entry to a course. This is, in part, an opportunity for you to make sure that you have covered the full checklist in preparing for your course, just to ensure that you really are in the right place for you. As importantly, it is also a way of allowing you to consider your next move. If you are going to move on to a further course (perhaps a PhD or developing a post-

8

graduate diploma into a masters course), you need to make the decision and begin the process relatively early in your current course. On a one-year course, for example, it is best to begin the process of applying for your next course after the first three to four months, to allow yourself enough time to research the course, make your application and, perhaps crucially, apply for funding.

▶ Becoming a postgraduate student

When you are applying to join a postgraduate course, or in the early stages of your course, there are several key points that you need to assess and act upon where necessary. These are listed below with some explanation of what to look for and how to move ahead.

Never assume that you are underqualified for a course

It is easy to assume that a course is beyond your reach simply because the course brochure gives a minimum entry requirement or a list of preferred qualifications. Do not be put off by this. Too many postgraduates are working through their second option course, feeling that in some way they failed even before they started, because they did not push themselves forward. If you have seen a course that really appeals to you, which you feel suits your experience and abilities precisely or will be most beneficial to your future career development, you should apply for the course. Remember that course brochures are only guidelines and entry requirements are rarely as rigid as they can at first appear. Universities and colleges want your business and, more importantly, they want good students who will bring value to a course and shine as a result of their skills and enthusiasm. Having said that, there is no point in simply applying for courses that seem to require qualifications that you do not have, without any explanation of your background and circumstances.

The most effective way to approach this is to contact the university or college directly. You might simply telephone and ask to speak to the course convenor about the possibility of joining the course (the course convenor is the lecturer responsible for running the course). If you feel less confident and would like to feel your way forward a little more cautiously, in the first instance speak to the course secretary. The secretaries usually know everything there is to know about the courses they help to administer, and your first phone call will allow you to discover how rigid the entry requirements are and how best you might apply. If you do not fit the standard model of a postgraduate student, you may be asked to attend an interview before you are accepted on a course, but this is to your advantage. It will give you the chance to discover more about the course, assess whether you could handle the workload involved and begin to develop a relationship with the course convenor, who may well be your supervisor if you develop your studying into a research project.

You can ease the process by doing the initial research as thoroughly as possible, so that you know all you need to about the course. Although it can seem daunting to face the task of applying for a course by making a direct approach such as this, it is far better than giving up on the opportunity simply because you do not possess the exact qualifications that you believe they want. Course convenors are quite used to receiving speculative calls about their courses from potential students, so spending some time talking you through the course and working out ways for you to join it will not be an inconvenience.

Check the course accreditation

If your course is a standard course run by a university, there will be no problem with accreditation. The university will stand by its course and give it full accreditation. If you are at another type of educational institution (or if your distance learning course is administered by an institution other than a university), you will need to make sure that the course is accredited in a meaningful way. This is usually the case, but it may not be overtly publicised. A college or academy course (or, in some circumstances, a new course run by a university) might be externally accredited by a university. This means that the university may have been involved in the creation of the course and will be overseeing its development; it will also monitor the results of the course to ensure that quality and academic rigour are maintained. If a course in which you are interested is not accredited by a university, this does not mean that you should dismiss it out of hand, but you do need to ensure that the qualification you will gain will be recognised in terms of both your future career and your academic development. The simple answer to this potential difficulty is just to ask.

The real problem here is that many postgraduates are hazy about accreditation. In most cases, by simply asking the question you will have resolved the issue. However, there is a more subtle element in the process of checking the validity and usefulness of your course. You are about to spend a lot of time, money and effort in undertaking a demanding course and it is desperately frustrating to find at its conclusion that, contrary to your expectations, it will not help you to move forward to where you want to be. Again, the solution is simple. If you hope to move on to a further postgraduate course, or if you intend to apply for membership of a professional or academic body on the basis of your course, it is essential to make sure before you become too embroiled that the qualification on offer will achieve this end. In this way you can work through your course confident that you are in the right place, doing the right course for your future.

Where your course might lead

If you already have a future career move or academic option in mind, it should be relatively simple for you to check the accreditation of your course and ensure that it will be seen as a valid qualification in helping you towards your ultimate destination. If you are less sure of your long-term plans (and this is the case for many postgraduates), it can be tempting simply to begin the course with little thought for the future. This is often the situation with postgraduates who have been away from a formal academic setting for some time. You are so relieved and excited to have been accepted on to a course, and the work itself is so interesting, that you feel no need to look beyond the end of the course. This need not be a problem, but postgraduate courses have a tendency to get you hooked. You begin a course, convinced that this is an isolated experience in your life, and then find yourself looking ahead to further opportunities, reluctant to give up on your academic development. So, the rule of thumb here is that, even if you do not intend to pursue your studying beyond your current course, it is advisable to look into other options. Could your postgraduate diploma course be developed into a masters course? Could the supervisor of your masters course help you to move on to a PhD? Is your continuing professional development course flexible enough to allow you to develop your research further in an area that is specific to your experience?

Finding a course, applying to join it and beginning the task of conquering the work can seem to be quite enough to be getting on with at this stage, and it is, but you will find that taking the time to look ahead and view your potential future will both encourage and reassure you as you move forward.

Learning outcomes

We tend not to think about specific learning outcomes when first embarking on a course. For some students, 'learning outcomes' is a phrase that is alien and means nothing, yet they are vital to your development in an academic context. Within some course outlines, you will see the learning outcomes for the course clearly defined. Look out for a phrase such as 'By the end of this course the student will be able to:' followed by a list of outcomes such as handling data, giving a presentation or analysing a text. Other course outlines will not mention learning outcomes as specifically as this, it will just be assumed that you can work out for yourself what your learning outcomes are likely to be. The potential problem with this is twofold. You might assume that you will achieve something that is important to you, and then find that the course does not offer you this outcome. Alternatively, the course convenors might be expecting you to undertake a series of tasks that offer you what you consider to be irrelevant or unnecessary learning outcomes.

Of course, you could simply ask the course convenor for a list of expected learning outcomes, but it is probably far more constructive to create your own list of desirable learning outcomes and then go back to the course literature or convenor to ascertain whether these can be achieved on the course. Some learning outcomes will be obvious, such as developing your statistical analysis skills or producing an independent piece of research; some are less so, such as enhancing your ability to debate a point in front of a group or analysing conflicting data in order to support a hypothesis. Your foundation skills base and areas for development will be discussed in some detail in Chapter 4, and from this you will be able to itemise the learning outcomes you would like to achieve. This will allow you to be specific about what you want from your course and you will then be able to identify the modules that are most useful to you and check whether they will run. It is rarely possible for a course convenor to guarantee that all optional modules will run, but if places are allocated on a 'first come, first served' basis you can make sure that you are at the head of the queue.

Flexibility

Although you will not want to begin studying with an expectation that things will go wrong, it is still a good idea to check how flexible the course and its teaching system might be. For example, if the course is part time and relies upon occasional face-to-face teaching sessions (perhaps weekend residential sessions or evening seminars), you will need to know in advance whether these sessions are a compulsory part of the course or an optional extra. You will, of course, still want to attend them, but you will know whether missing them, if this is sometimes unavoidable, is going to be a major problem. Similarly, if you are studying via distance or open learning, you may assume that the timescale of the course will be highly flexible, yet in reality inflexible deadlines might be imposed and you will need to take this into account as you plan your working pattern.

The other principal area in which you might need some flexibility is the overall length of your course. Whilst you will have in mind a period of time over which you intend to study (perhaps one year full time for a masters course or two years part time for a postgraduate diploma), and this will be the timescale imposed to some extent by your university or college, things can go awry. Work or personal commitments might throw you off course, or you might discover that one element of your course (an industrial placement, for instance) cannot be organised as quickly as you had hoped. You will need to confirm at the outset that you can go on studying beyond the expected timescale and still remain within the framework of the course, and you will also need to consider the cost implications of this. It may be that you have to pay an extra year's tuition fees if you run over time and you need to be aware of this.

Other aspects of your course in which you might need some flexibility can usually be assessed as the course progresses, but they are worth mentioning here. Can you change your personal tutor relatively easily if you have a problem? Will a supervisor be imposed on you as you develop your research or can you negotiate to get the supervisor of your choice? Can you change to a different seminar group if you find the timing of one seminar course difficult? Can you change from a part-time to a full-time course (or vice versa) if your circumstances change? Can an extended piece of research be replaced by two shorter projects? Can group presentations be replaced by individual presentations if you find it difficult to arrange to get together with a team outside your set studying hours? I am not suggesting here that you face your first meeting with your personal tutor or supervisor armed with a long list of questions and demands, but it is worth writing down a list of your individual learning needs and the ways in which your circumstances might impact upon your course so that you can foresee potential problems.

Doing the research

A university or college prospectus is just the first port of call as you research postgraduate courses. It is best not to be too swayed by a glossy brochure; it may accurately reflect the institution and the course, but it may be covering up hidden disadvantages. You will also need to access the website so that you can get a feel for the institution as a whole, rather than just learning about one course. It is also worth finding out the career destinations of previous postgraduates from your chosen course (this information might be offered under the Careers Advisory Service section on the website). If you can, try also to access any study chat rooms related to the course that you would like to do and any online tutorial websites. You may need an access password for this, but such sites may offer the facility to allow visitors to view the site for a limited period, just to see what is happening on the course.

Other websites will also be of value to you. Rather than sticking with the official website, see if you can find any websites related to the institution or that mention it. You can type in either the name of the institution or the name of the course and let the search engine do the work for you. You might discover an independent assessment site offering an evaluation of your course or a range of institutions offering similar courses. This need not confuse your choice, it will simply allow you to compare what is on offer on your chosen course with similar courses held elsewhere. A brochure will give you the facts about a course and try to sell it to you; the course convenor and secretary can give you some of the inside information that may sway your decision; the websites may tip the balance.

Funding

Even if you suspect that you do not have the remotest chance of getting funding for your studying, it is still worth looking into funding options. These will vary according to your area of study, but you will need to explore avenues such as public funding by nationally recognised funding bodies, cheap loans as part of a career development plan, funding direct from the institution at which you are studying (including access or hardship grants and loans), commercial sponsorship and private educational charities. You can find out about some of these potential funding sources via the Internet, but you would also do well to visit the Careers Advisory Service or research and funding department of the institution at which you intend to study and your local library for detailed guides.

If you are already on a course and are a self-funding student, there is no reason to suppose that you will never be eligible for funding. It may not be too late to apply for some backdated help if your circumstances and course fit into the criteria of institutional or central funding. If your circumstances change and you need financial help, tell your personal tutor and you will be given help to access a hardship fund or longer term financing. If you are funding yourself on an initial postgraduate course and would like to move on to a further course, you may then fall into the category of students who are funded. Some universities offer scholarships or studentships to selected postgraduates who have already proved their worth and staying power by successfully completing an initial postgraduate course. There is no need to be put off by the terms 'scholarship' (sounds rather high flying) or 'studentship' (sounds like it should be for undergraduates). There is a limited amount of money available and there is no point in missing out on your share of it simply because you assumed that you were not eligible. This happens surprisingly often, but you can make sure that you do not lose out.

An established course

It is usually difficult to tell from a course brochure whether a course has been running for some time or is in its infancy. Most postgraduates do not think to ask the question, but it is useful to know the answer. If a course is well established, you can be sure that lecturers and tutors will be well versed in what to do and how to handle queries, and that the course will have had a chance to build up a reputation in your field. On the other hand, a well-established course might have tutors who are rather set in their ways, administration that is not very flexible and an outlook that is rather traditional.

If a course is new (perhaps in its first couple of years of existence), potentially you have the opposite situation. The lecturers and tutors might be more open to new ways of working within the course, willing to try new ideas as to what can be covered and flexible in their attitude towards recruiting students onto the course. On the downside, the course and its administration and running will not be tried and tested and there will be no track record for the course, so no established reputation with which to impress future employers or course convenors.

These are, of course, generalisations and it is unlikely that you will have any firm preference for either an established or a new course, but if you know how long a course has been running, this fact might combine with other factors in helping you to choose between courses. If you are applying for a vocational course that will lead to professional accreditation, it is also advisable to check that there are no planned legislative or regulatory changes that would undermine the professional value of the course.

First find your expert

This is perhaps a counsel of perfection, given that you will not be faced with an endless stream of course options. You know the area in which you want to study, the course profile and logistics that will suit you, so your choice is largely made for you. If yours is mainly a taught course, you will be offered lectures and seminars by a variety of experts in the field and you will receive the benefit of this breadth of experience. If, however, your course is largely research-based, you might want to proceed with more care. The reputation of a university or college will lead you to it in the first place, but try to find out about the research interests and publications of the lecturer who you will be allocated as a supervisor. The relationship with your supervisor will be the most crucial aspect of your research course, so it is vital that, if possible, you do some research about potential supervisors. It is tempting, of course, to apply to the most prestigious university or college running a course that seems suited to your needs and qualifications, but if you then find yourself with a supervisor who has little experience in your field, you might be disappointed in the level of expert supervision you receive. This relationship is discussed in more depth in Chapter 5, but your first task is to make sure that the institution to which you are applying has an expert suitable to your needs, with the time to supervise you, or someone with related interests who will be enthusiastic about expanding his or her knowledge base as your research progresses.

▶ Assessment

The means by which you will be assessed might be one of your criteria in choosing a postgraduate course. With this in mind, the list below will help you to focus on how the varying methods of assessment might impact upon your learning patterns by explaining how they tend to work, what might be expected of you and how you can ensure that you are on top of assessment throughout your course. As with the course structures outlined in Chapter 1, you may find yourself faced with a mixture of these assessment methods, but you can be confident that the assessment with which you will be involved will fall into one or more of the following four broad categories: examinations; coursework; continuous assessment; and extended independent research.

Examinations

For many students one of the most appealing aspects of a postgraduate course is their belief that they will be able to say goodbye to examinations forever. This may well be the case, but it is worth remembering that some postgraduate courses are still assessed primarily by examination. It may be, for example, that the taught part of your course is assessed in this way prior to you moving on to an extended piece of research, or that you are asked to pass a foundation examination before moving on to the principal modules of your course. There are several key points to bear in mind if you find that your course includes some assessment by examination.

Be brave

Even if you hate examinations, or have had bad experiences in the past, try not to let yourself be put off a whole course simply because there is an element of assessment by examination. A postgraduate examination is likely to feel very different from an undergraduate or school examination. You will be more in control because you have chosen this subject and have carried out your own research into the area of work on which you are being examined. You are older, more able to cope with the stress and will have the chance to improve your examination techniques in advance of the assessment.

Examination workshops

Universities and colleges are becoming increasingly enthusiastic about study skills workshops and you will have the opportunity to attend them well in advance of your examinations. These workshops will give you the chance to improve your revision technique, control your nerves and reduce your stress levels in order to work through examinations more effectively. Even if you are not going to be assessed by examinations, workshops such as these can still be useful to you. If you view your research project as an extended form of examination, workshops dealing with time management, stress reduction and revision techniques can all help you to manage your research successfully.

Think beyond the examinations
It is unlikely that your entire postgraduate course will be assessed by examination, so it is important that you place this one form of assessment in context within the broader requirements of your course. It might be, for example, that you will be assessed by examination in the early part of your course so that your progress can be checked prior to moving on. In this case it is essential to grasp the bigger picture and see examinations for what they are: simply one piece, probably a relatively minor piece, in the jigsaw of assessment. Once you can visualise examinations in this way, you will find them far more manageable.

What examinations are designed to achieve
Examinations at pre-university level are designed to elicit a series of facts from students, combined with a requirement to show some independent thinking about what they have learned. Undergraduate examinations are similar, although they are obviously set at a higher level and more credit will be given to original ideas and a more sophisticated approach to each subject area. Postgraduate examinations are more diverse and your response to them will vary according to what each examination is designed to achieve. In the early stages of a heavily fact-based course, you may simply be asked to prove that you have command of all the necessary data in order to proceed. In a course that is principally concerned with concepts and ideologies, you will be asked to think more widely, see patterns as they emerge and include far more of your own ideas in your answers. It is important that you find out as early as possible what type of examination you are going to face. By understanding what is being asked of you, you will be able to develop strategies for success that will reduce your anxiety about examinations.

The examination structure
There are several examination structures that your university or college might choose to use. Multiple choice examinations assess your command of the facts efficiently and quickly. Short answer examinations allow you to show how you would develop an argument in defence of your position. Essay questions require that you expand your arguments and demonstrate a relatively high level of understanding and articulation. If you find out what type of examination structure you will be working within, you can get to grips with the preparation, confident in what you are aiming to achieve. Do not forget that self-assessment might take the place of the more traditional examination in your course, particularly if it is an open or distance learning course. This form of assessment might take place on hard copy or over the Internet and has the advantage of potentially reducing your stress level, as you will be working within your normal work space and, in some cases, with

a relatively loose timeframe within which to work. Self-assessment such as this may not be designed as a gateway through to the next part of your course; it may be used far more as a backup to your studying, a way of allowing you to monitor your progress as your course develops.

Timing

If the examinations on your course are designed to monitor your progress from the earliest stages of your studying, you might be undertaking your first assessment within the first few weeks of your course. Although this might seem daunting, it is actually advantageous from your point of view. It will get you into the swing of things from the outset, help you to overcome any examination anxiety that you might have, by requiring you to face this challenge so early, and give you useful feedback on your progress. If your examinations are later in the course, you will have more time to work towards them, but in either case you will have to ensure that you are clear about when the assessment is to take place, so that you can timetable your revision around your other tasks, including any independent research projects that you are undertaking. Time management is considered in Chapter 6, and revision planning will form part of that discussion. At this early stage in your studying, it is a good idea to find out not only about the timing of examinations, but also the practicalities of retakes. You will not, of course, want to think about the possibility of failing before you even begin, but it is sensible at least to know whether retakes are possible (they are likely to be) and when they will be held. You can then put this thought to one side, safe in the knowledge that you have this fail-safe position if things go awry.

Coursework

Whilst you might be faced with examinations, or self-assessment tests, as part of your course, it is more common for postgraduates to be assessed by coursework. This might take the form of continuous assessment or extended independent research, discussed below, but it might be relatively highly supervised, with each piece of coursework reflecting just one part of your course. In a masters course, for example, you might be expected to produce a series of assessed essays or reports of several thousand words in length, followed by a more extended dissertation to complete the course. In a PhD course, you might be asked to produce interim pieces of work (which may or may not be formally assessed) in order that your progress as an academic can be monitored.

Limited pieces of supervised coursework are unlikely to be produced in isolation. Essays might be written as a result of work in specific seminars or as a way of completing a module. You may be given the opportunity to produce a draft essay or a plan that is then open to constructive criticism by your tutor or supervisor, especially if it is produced early in your course. You may be in a position to reproduce some version of this work as part of your final dissertation or thesis. As you can see, the coursework system tends to be flexible, often well supported and useful to you, both in terms of assessing your progress and developing your research, analytical, organisational and writing skills. Coursework is therefore not something to be feared, but rather an opportunity to be used fully in order to support your studying.

Continuous assessment

This may take the form of coursework essays or reports, but it might also involve methods of assessment with which you are less familiar. You might be expected, for example, to give formal, professional-level presentations on topics with which you are engaged or give interim verbal reports on your research project. You might also be asked to produce reports on work-based projects or devise and discuss data-gathering methods and statistical analyses. Self-assessment via the Internet might be crucial to your success. If your postgraduate course is part of your professional life, you might be assessed on your professional activities, being asked to analyse your approach and suggest ways in which you could further develop your skills. In practical courses, such as science and technology, your laboratory work, research and other practical projects will be assessed.

The key here is to work not only on the content of the assessed work but also on its delivery. You know that you can handle the work, but is your presentation technique going to be assessed? What percentage of marks will be allocated to the form and style of presentation? If you are to give a verbal report on your work, who will be listening to you? Will there be a question and answer session? Are you expected to ask your audience for guidance on how to proceed in your research? If you are devising methods of data-gathering and statistical analysis, will you be expected to develop these methods further and use them in your future research projects? If self-assessment plays a part in your course, will your results be tracked by your tutors at every stage? If you are to be assessed on your professional activities, will this assessment be carried out by fellow professionals in your area or will you have to tailor your report or presentation to academics outside your field? If practical projects or laboratory work are to form part of your assessment, how much time will you have to prepare? Are you fully aware of the health and safety implications of the work you intend to undertake? Will you be able to retake practicals if things go wrong? This might seem like a long list of variables, but you need to know as early as possible exactly what is involved in each form of continuous assessment. The advantage of this method of assessment is that you get regular feedback and know that you are succeeding in your course at each stage, and once you understand what is involved you can master each form of assessment as it becomes due.

Extended independent research

This is, of course, the type of assessment most often associated with post-graduate work. There is plenty of advice throughout this book on how to tackle independent research, but there are two aspects of research projects that it is a good idea to bear in mind initially. Firstly, make sure that you are clear about the word length of your research project. This may sound obvious, but the length varies widely from course to course and hearsay or past experience is unlikely to help you. It is common for masters dissertations to be 20,000 words, for example, but 30,000 is also common. A PhD thesis might be 90,000 words, but in some cases there will be no word limit (although this is relatively rare). There are advantages and disadvantages to each word length, so there is no need to be put off whatever it turns out to be, but at the outset of your course you do need to know exactly how long your research project will be. One thing is certain: however many words you are asked to produce, by the end of your research there will never be enough to incorporate everything that you now want to include.

The second aspect of your research that you need to be clear about is the timing of the project. It might, for example, be designed as an 'add-on' to a taught course, in which case you may be given an almost unlimited amount of time in which to complete it (although, as already mentioned, there may be cost implications to extending your studying over too long a time period). It might be that you are given strict time limits on completion, and failure to complete on time in these cases can have fairly dire consequences (you might, for example, be unable to graduate for a further six months if you do not submit on time). In a closely supervised course, producing your extended piece of research might be a cumulative process, with a section to be produced each term or half term, and only the final collation and checking to be carried out in the final stages of your course. Clearly, your experience as a postgraduate is going to be influenced greatly by the way in which your extended piece of research is timed, so understanding how it will work and being clear about requirements and deadlines is going to be vital.

Supervision

Chapter 5 is devoted entirely to this important issue, but you will need to understand how this relationship works at the beginning of your course. The idea of having a supervisor to guide you through your postgraduate course may be alien to you, but you will soon get used to the system and appreciate its benefits. At this stage, there are three questions that you need to ask. Firstly, will you be able to choose your supervisor? If you are on a course where you can spend a little time developing your ideas about an extended research project, you might not be allocated a supervisor until you begin work on the project, when you will receive supervision from a lecturer who is familiar with your field. If your course is more firmly delineated from its early stages, you might be allocated a supervisor at the outset. Neither of these situations need be a problem to you, but it is a good idea to discover whether your view will have any impact upon the allocation of a supervisor. If this is the case, you can bear it in mind as you develop relationships with lecturers. Secondly, you will want to know whether you will work under the supervision of several academics or just one. Both systems have advantages. If you are to be supervised by one person throughout your course, you will gain the benefit of a continuing and productive relationship with an expert who knows your strengths and recognises your weaknesses and can help you accordingly. On the other hand, if you are to have a series of supervisors (perhaps one for each area of research or module of your course), you will be able to rely on the support of academics with a range of expertise and approaches to your work.

The third issue that you will want to address is the level of supervision you can expect to receive. Try to find out what is usual on your course, as levels of supervision vary depending upon the type of course and between individual supervisors. Some supervisors see their postgraduate students on a weekly basis and expect to set assignments and discuss progress at each meeting. Others would be surprised to see their students more than twice a term. This does not mean that the former type of supervisor is necessarily any more dedicated than the latter, but this is going to be a key factor in how you work with your supervisor, and so may impact upon your choice of supervisor, if you are given a level of preference. Even if you have a wonderful supervisor, with inspirational ideas and supportive methods of working, this will be of little use to you if you know that you need the discipline and support of a weekly meeting and your supervisor only expects to see you at the beginning and end of each term. Similarly, if you would prefer to work on your own, giving yourself time to expand your thoughts and work through your research in relative isolation, a weekly supervision could be restrictive and stifling. You can begin to feel that your supervisions are intruding upon your working pattern in a negative way and this can be a difficult problem to resolve. It is far easier to find a supervisor who will support your working pattern than to try to work with a supervisor whose approach is very different from your own.

You might feel, by the end of these opening chapters, that there is a lot to think about even before you get stuck into your course. In fact, many of the issues discussed so far are more in the nature of a checklist than anything you need to work on in depth at this stage of your studying. It is useful for you to be aware of all the options available to postgraduates, even if only some of these are open to you, as in this way you can assess the value of your course, understand the ways in which its structure might affect your working pattern and begin to devise strategies to meet the challenges ahead. Many new postgraduates give no thought to the level of supervision they might receive during their research or the ways in which they might be assessed, and there is simply too little time on your course to allow you to find these things out by default, by which time it might be too late to improve your situation.

By understanding the learning environment in which you will be studying and taking control, as far as you are able, of some of the variables in your study programme, you will be in a stronger position to complete your course successfully. Once you have worked through the issues raised in these chapters, you will be free to concentrate your time and energies on the specifics of your course, the learning opportunities open to you, the skills that you can develop and the research that will be one of the most satisfying aspects of your postgraduate experience. It is to the first of these that we will turn next.

Your postgraduate experience is an exciting challenge, made up of a series of studying opportunities, each of which brings its own challenges and rewards. This chapter will have given you an idea of the range of elements that might make up your course and shown you some of the ways in which you can make the most of them. If you succeed in maximising the studying opportunities available to you and exploiting each element of your course, you will be en route to managing your life as a postgraduate.

Spot guide

Key points to remember from this chapter:

- never assume that you are underqualified for a course
- make sure that your chosen course has full and meaningful accreditation
- try not to overlook the future possibilities that might arise from your course
- identify specific learning outcomes that you need to achieve
- if you have many demands upon your time, make sure that your course is flexible
- do your research: find out as much as you can about your course in advance
- even if you do not think that you will get it, still look into applying for funding
- find an expert in your field and make sure that he or she can supervise your research
- never be put off by any form of assessment; instead, learn what is involved on your course
- get help if you need it in examination techniques
- think about supervision even before you begin your extended research

3 Studying Opportunities

Troubleshooting guide

Read this chapter for help in the following areas:

- if you want to know how postgraduate seminars work
- if you want to make the most of lectures
- if you are expecting a visiting speaker or guest lecturer on your course
- if you are unsure about whether to attend an academic conference
- if you would like to be involved in a postgraduate discussion group
- if you have to attend tutorials
- if you are confused by technology and e-learning and want to know more
- if you have ever thought about a postgraduate placement
- if you will have to carry out work-based projects
- if you intend to study abroad

Working in a fog of confusion is the worst possible way to tackle a post-graduate course, yet sometimes you might feel as if you cannot help but be confused. This is not necessarily because you are unsure about your subject or your area of research – these will probably be clear to you – it is because you are unclear about the demands that will be made upon your time and the input that will be expected of you. It can feel as if all sorts of demands are being placed upon your work schedule and it is not always made clear to postgraduates how these activities will support their work, which elements are compulsory and which are optional and the level of involvement required of you. The best way to approach this is to see each scheduled activity as a learning opportunity. If you begin in this positive way, asking what you can get out of each aspect of your course, you will find it easier to cope and max-imise those studying opportunities. In this chapter, the most common studying opportunities open to postgraduates will be explored and the ways in which you can tackle each one will be explained. Not all these course elements will necessarily be available to you, but most will become familiar as your course progresses.

▶ Seminars

What is involved

Postgraduate seminars are, in key respects, very different from undergraduate seminars, so even if you have come straight from a degree course, you might feel a little wrong-footed when you come to face your first postgraduate seminar. In essence, seminars are discussion groups, led by a tutor, intended to bring together postgraduates in the same field to discuss aspects of their subject and their common objectives. Seminars are run even if the postgraduates on a course all intend to pursue different areas of research in their dissertations. They might be held weekly, sometimes for just part of the course, or they may be more sporadic. Running seminars is a way of bringing a postgraduate group together and providing a cohesive core to a course. They are useful to you, not because each week's subject is necessarily going to be of great importance to your research, but because they allow you to explore a wide range of fields related to your core subject.

If you are being asked to complete several assessed pieces of coursework prior to your dissertation or thesis, you will use the seminars as starting points in your work. In a series of seminars you may view several as being of general interest but not covering themes that you intend to develop, whilst several more will be sufficiently relevant to your area of interest to allow you to work up the ideas presented in them in order to produce your coursework.

You might be surprised at how small postgraduate seminars can be. It is not unheard of for a postgraduate seminar to run with only two or three students, which can be unnerving at first. You might be expecting to join a group of a dozen or so students (as would be usual with an undergraduate seminar) and then find yourself sitting with a tutor and just one or two colleagues. This leaves the spotlight on you, which is not the easiest situation to face when you begin your course and are perhaps a little unsure of your ground. As time moves on, you will come to enjoy the opportunity this offers, as you will at the very least receive lots of individual attention, so try not to be too put off if you are in a very small group – the hints given below should help you to cope.

The second surprise can come with the level of contribution that is expected of you in a seminar. As you settle into your course, it is quite possible for you to make minimum preparations for a seminar in an area you do not intend to pursue, perhaps just by reading the extracts, articles or reports that you have been given in advance. However, you will still be asked at *all* seminars to contribute as fully as possible to the discussion. This is no longer a situation in which you can hope to hide behind your colleagues and simply try to look interested, you are now in a position where your contribution will be expected and valued in a new way. Rather than a tutor using a seminar as another lecturing opportunity, during which you can sit and take notes, a postgraduate seminar is a meeting of academics, colleagues who each have an equal and valid contribution to make. The tutor might begin the discussion, even lead the group through the area to be covered, but you will be expected to do most of the work.

The third way in which postgraduate seminars differ from undergraduate or professional seminars is that each one is likely to focus upon the possibility of research. So, rather than simply talking around a subject and gathering information, you will be expected to explore ways in which you might, if you have an interest in the area, develop it into a research project, either for assessed coursework or for a dissertation or thesis. This places a different emphasis on a postgraduate seminar. You will be discussing a subject area, you will expect to receive information, but, crucially, you will also be expected to ask research questions. How much research has already been carried out on this area? Is there plenty of primary material available? Can you contact experts in this field relatively easily? Does your seminar tutor have a particular expertise in this subject? How might you structure your research? This new aspect of seminars is often overlooked by postgraduates, particularly in the early stages of their courses, and can lead to missed opportunities.

How to make the most of them

- Seminars can disorientate students because they might be held sporadically, so make sure that you know when each of your seminars is to be held.
- Although lectures will be valuable to you, seminars are your key chance to develop your ideas; in this way they are the most important building block in your course, so be ready to join in each seminar discussion.
- If you know that you will be absent from a seminar, let your tutor know. If the seminar group is small, it may be possible to alter its timing. Even in a large group your absence will be noticed, so letting your tutor know if you will be absent is a sensible move to make.
- Success in seminars is all about preparation. Even if all you can do is read the bare minimum of the material set for discussion, you will still

be able to join in. Do not give in to the temptation to miss a seminar because you have done only minimal preparation, it is rarely worth it.

- Even if you have little interest in the topic to be discussed at a seminar, still turn up and join in. At the very least you can discard the topic, confident that you have explored it as a possibility. At the most, you might find new ideas for your research, new ways of working or novel insights into your own research methodology.

- Seminars are time-savers from your point of view. The tutor (and your fellow postgraduates) will be able to offer interesting ideas about your area of work, tell you about books you have not yet heard of and give you suggestions about where to go next. This information is not readily accessible elsewhere and is easily forgotten after the seminar, so take as many notes as you can during the session.

- Try to view each seminar as the start of a journey. If something that is said in a seminar rings a bell for you, it could be the beginning of a brilliant idea, so make a note of who made the point that interests you, and make sure that you have the email addresses of everyone at the seminar, including the tutor. You will have this list for your regular contacts, of course, but it is frustrating to join a seminar group led by a guest lecturer or share a seminar with visiting students and then not be able to contact them easily in the future.

▶ Lectures

What is involved

Many postgraduate courses are lecture-based, but you might be tempted to view them as optional, to scan the lecture list and decide which lectures to attend. This is not a good idea. Although inevitably not every lecture will hold your interest throughout, and some lectures may cover areas that will not form part of your coursework or research project, they will still be useful to you. They give you the opportunity to get to know lecturers who you might not otherwise meet. They allow you to consider new ways of viewing your specialist area by reference to other subjects, and you will hear mention of primary material and secondary sources that might not be on any of your reference lists but are highly relevant to your research.

How to make the most of them

- If you have no lectures scheduled on your course, do not assume that there are no lectures available for you to attend. Your university or college will run a wide variety of courses, most with lectures, and these may be of value to you. No lecturer is likely to object to you attending one lecture in a series and most will be flattered by your interest. If you are not clear about what is on offer, there are several ways to make sure that you do not miss out. Check out the website for courses that are running, as lecture schedules might be included. Wander around different departments (including your own) and pick up lecture lists and reading lists that might be relevant. Departmental secretaries are very knowledgeable about the courses they help to run, so talking to them will give you clues about lectures that might be of interest to you.

- If you attend a lecture given by a lecturer who you find inspiring, there is no need to discount this useful contact simply because the lecture you attended did not focus upon your primary area of research. Make contact after the lecture, either in person or via email, explain your interest and see if you can develop a useful working relationship for the future.

- If you are attending a particularly dull lecture (it can happen), try not to see the whole experience as wasted. Some of your best ideas will come to you as your mind wanders around the subject being discussed. Keep an ear on the lecture (it might become interesting or a writer might be mentioned whose work is relevant to you) but also allow your mind to relax in a controlled way. You should still be focused on the subject area, but you can think simultaneously about your coursework, dissertation or thesis (you might want to carry an outline plan around with you) and jot down ideas as they come to you. As you revisit your notes during your course, you will find that some of your best work arises from these ideas captured in the margins of your lecture notes.

- If you have a heavily lecture-based course and you know that you will not be able to attend every lecture, pair up as early as possible with another student with a similar problem so that you can share lecture notes whenever one of you has to miss a lecture.

- View your lectures as useful markers in the structure of your course. It is all too easy to find yourself isolated during a postgraduate course as you spend so much time working on your individual research projects. If you make a point of attending lectures, it will help you to feel involved in your course, give you time away from your computer and the library and offer you the perfect chance to meet up with your fellow postgraduates after the lecture.

▶ **Visiting speakers**

What is involved

Visiting speakers are an attractive option for postgraduate course convenors. By inviting in outside speakers, they can bring the latest research to you, introduce you to experts in your specialist field and show you how academics work through their subjects. Visits by outside experts are usually structured on a fairly formal basis. They will usually begin by the speaker giving a paper. This involves the speaker reading from a prepared script, perhaps a chapter from his or her latest book or a paper (lecture) written especially for the visit to you. It can be quite an odd experience when first you hear someone 'give a paper'. Rather than interacting with you, the speaker might simply be reading the paper through, with few asides and no interaction with the audience. It is only after the paper has been given that speaker and audience engage in any discussion. This might be relatively formal, with your convenor asking for questions and giving a time limit to the discussion. It might be far less formal, with the speaker simply asking for your comments.

This sounds simple enough, but in fact it can be intimidating to be faced with a call for questions. The silence lengthens and you are desperately searching for something original, relevant and intelligent to say. This can be made even more intimidating if the event has been advertised widely and you are in a room with plenty of unfamiliar faces, several of whom you suspect belong to senior lecturers. In reality, of course, the onus to ask questions will not rest solely with you (however much it can feel like this at the time) and your convenor is bound to have a set of prepared questions in case the silence lengthens to unbearable proportions. You will get used to these events and they are of great value to you if you learn how to exploit them.

How to make the most of them

- Unlike seminars, you will not have to do much preparation for most guest speakers, although you might want to read some of their work if the subject under discussion is of particular interest to you.
- If you are concerned about what questions to ask, there are two ways to tackle the situation. You can simply think of a very open question in advance of the session, so that you can relax whilst you listen to the paper, knowing you have a question ready. Alternatively, you can be thinking of a relevant question as the paper opens, note it down as it comes to you and then sit back and enjoy the rest of the paper.
- You are not being tested here. It is perfectly acceptable simply to listen to the paper, ask no questions and just make notes that are relevant to you.
- If you have a question to ask that is very specific to your work, which you feel will be of little interest to other members of the group, do not be put off asking it altogether. There is usually time allowed after the session when the speaker will loiter, waiting to answer questions from

anyone who did not want to ask a specific question in the general discussion.

- As with lecturers, make sure that you have email addresses for guest speakers, just in case you find their work relevant to your research at a later stage.
- Look around the audience. Is there anyone present who you feel you should make contact with? Will there be a chance to socialise after the event? Can you network effectively?
- Remember that you might well be listening to a 'work in progress'. This is not the finished article or completed chapter of a book, but a draft of what the speaker might choose to commit to print. As such, your comments really will be valued. Queries that you have and points that you make will have an impact upon the finished product. This is a further example of how postgraduate work differs from the undergraduate experience. You are now an academic amongst colleagues and your experience and expertise will be respected.
- If you find speakers fascinating, find out where next you might hear them speak. Is there a conference at which they will be giving a paper? Do they run lecture courses that you might be able to attend? Do they run websites supporting their research? Increasing the usefulness of the event by extending the opportunity for contact and input into your research is the best way to make the most of guest speakers.

► Conferences

What is involved

It is relatively unusual for undergraduates to attend conferences, although you may have attended several in your professional life. In structure, academic conferences do not differ greatly from any other form of conference. They consist of a series of speakers giving papers, with time for questions and answers following the conclusion of the paper, and sometimes also a series of discussion sessions.

There are two fundamental obstacles to getting the most out of academic conferences. The first is that they sometimes seem to be well-kept secrets. Publicity is often sparse as they are run on restricted budgets, so the only way you might hear of them is to ensure that you are on academic mailing lists. The second is that they are not a series of presentations, but rather a series of papers. This is quite different from the style of presenting at commerical or professional conferences, where the aim is to keep the audience engaged, sell them an idea or motivate them. It can be disconcerting to find yourself watching an academic speaking about an area of mutual interest, who fails to make eye contact (the speaker will probably be looking down at the paper he or she is reading) and expects no audience reaction until the conclusion of the paper. Of course, this is a generalisation. Some academic papers are given with real flair, plenty of eye contact, a feeling that the speaker is really engaging with the audience and a plethora of slides or hand-outs to support the arguments being put forward. However, if you are used to PowerPoint presentations by dynamic speakers whose role is to motivate the audience, be prepared for the possibility of a very different experience.

How to make the most of them

- Find out about as many conferences as you can. Check notice boards and the doors of lecturers' offices for posters and make sure that you ask visiting speakers about conferences at which they intend to speak.
- Ask your supervisor or course convenor about academic mailing lists. Are there lists that would be relevant to you? You need only be on two or three to find out most of what is going on in your area. Once you are on one list you will find that you receive information from a variety of study groups.
- Be selective. It is worth attending several conferences during your course just for the experience of being part of an academic occasion and to boost your list of contacts, but it can be expensive to travel to a conference and pay your conference fee, so try to find the conferences that are most relevant to you. Remember that attending even one conference will help to calm your nerves if you are later asked to give a paper at a conference.
- If the cost of attending a conference is prohibitive or it clashes with your other commitments, find out if the conference proceedings (that is, the contents of the papers, reports of discussions and details of publications arising from the conference) are to be lodged on the Internet. They may take a little time to appear, but it is worth checking out the possibility of gaining the benefits of the conference via the Internet if you cannot attend.
- See academic conferences as fact-finding missions. If you really work at it, you will find out during meals breaks about unpublished research in your field, further conferences to be held and primary sources that you have overlooked. You might also, if you are lucky, hear about funding opportunities.
- Learn to ask open questions. If you want to know more about an area, but are concerned about how to frame the question, make it as general as possible to allow the speaker to discourse more widely on one aspect of the subject.
- Although this is not a formal lecture situation, make notes as if it were.

Your notes will most usefully include references to academics you have not yet heard about, books you have not yet read and new ideas about how to approach your subject.

- As with lectures, try to see each paper as an opportunity. It need not be of direct relevance to you to be of value. It might be that just one aside by the speaker will open up a whole new area of research to you.

▶ Discussion groups

What is involved

Discussion groups are similar to seminar groups, but they tend to involve students from a wider range of subjects and departments. They might be a formal element of your course, although they will not always be supervised by a tutor. They are sometimes led by students, each taking a turn to discourse upon, and lead a disucssion on, a particular subject. They are intended to support interdisciplinary work between subject areas and allow for networking between students and departments. They might be held as open discussions or be more formal in structure, with a paper or presentation followed by a disucsssion. Although they are sometimes subject-specific, they can be at their most beneficial if they are held to discuss general aspects of the postgraduate experience, such as how to create a bibliography or get your work published, and are led by experienced researchers or lecturers.

How to make the most of them

- If you get the chance, volunteer to lead one of these sessions. They can be useful opportunities to meet with lecturers and you will want to show that you are involved in your course and energetic in your approach.
- If a session covers a subject of particular interest to you, prepare in advance. Time passes swiftly in these sessions, so be prepared to guide the discussion into your area of research.
- If you find that time is running short, make sure that you can contact each member of the group in the future.
- You will be surprised at who turns up to these sessions. They are often held in lunchtime breaks so lecturers can just drop in to listen to the discussion, but you might never meet them in a more formal setting, so do not be afraid to approach them directly to get their email addresses.
- Try to support the rest of your group if you can. If you think that a discussion session will not be of great value to you, it might be worth

turning up simply to make sure that whoever is leading the session can see a friendly face: they will return the favour when it is your turn to lead.

- If discussion groups have not been set up on your course, consider beginning one yourself. It can be very informal and need not meet more than twice a term or so, but you will find it beneficial if you can get something along these lines going for your study group.

▶ Tutorials

What is involved

The term 'tutorials' is used differently between universities, so you might find that what have been described above as seminars are referred to as tutorials on your course (particularly if you are on a science- or technology-based postgraduate course). Alternatively, tutorials within your institution might be meetings with your coursework marker, designed to discuss a specific piece of work. You might also attend tutorials (or supervisions) with your supervisor to discuss your progress in more general terms, and these will be discussed in detail in Chapter 5. In this section, the focus will be upon meeting with lecturers to discuss specific pieces of coursework, essays or research. You could be asked to read your work aloud, which might be an unfamiliar experience for you, or you might be asked to join with another postgraduate who shares your field of interest and has produced a piece of work in an area similar to your own.

Tutorials can be a real challenge to new postgraduates. You might fear that you will be on trial, asked to analyse your work and defend your position to an unfamiliar lecturer, put on the spot about your knowledge base and research methodology. In reality, tutorials offer a fantastic chance to expand your view of your subject, get expert help in your field and develop your ideas as a researcher.

How to make the most of them

- As with so much else, the secret is to be prepared, but try not to be over-prepared. It is useful to read over your piece of work before you attend a tutorial, but there is little value in poring over every word, worrying that you might be challenged on each point you have made.
- There is no need to be nervous about tutorials. Easier to say than to do, but if you can view them as opportunities to broaden your area of knowledge and analyse your approach, you will be in a better position to make the most of them.
- If you cannot attend a tutorial, contact the marker and make another

appointment. This is unlikely to cause a problem and will ensure that you do not miss out on the chance to discuss your work.

- If you are concerned about a piece of work, feel that you have not achieved your best or are disappointed with the written comments the marker has made, you will naturally be inclined to want to avoid any disucsssion of the work. Instead, be courageous and face the tutorial with an open mind. Your work will not be a complete disaster. Perhaps you have tried an approach that did not work (better now than in your final dissertation or thesis), been unaware of facts that are relevant (you have time to get to grips with them) or overlooked some vital piece of research (you cannot know everything). No problem will be insoluble and the tutor is there to help you to move forward.
- If you are unclear about how the tutorial will run (how long will it be? Will you be asked to read your work? Will you be paired with another student?), try to find out in advance rather than worrying about it. You could email the tutor concerned or talk to the departmental secretary, who will probably know how each particular tutor likes to run tutorials.
- The ideal situation is that you leave the tutorial feeling absolutely clear about what has been discussed and confident about your next move. If you are unsure about what is being said, try to get clarification there and then, but if you are still unsure by the end of the tutorial, do not leave issues unresolved. It is better to email the tutor, or ask for a further meeting once you have done some more research, rather than leave threads of ideas tangled or methods of approaching your subject only partially understood. They may not be important in themselves, but they can undermine you as you continue with your research and this is never going to be a productive way to move forward.

▶ E-learning

What is involved

You will probably be the sort of person who either loves technology or loathes it, but, whichever category you fall into, you will come to appreciate the value of information technology within your postgraduate course. Modules are usually supported by software programs that allow lecturers to place course information on web pages, along with reading lists, self-assessment tests and seminar material. This is particularly true of modules that are general in nature, such as those designed to help you to manage your research, write a dissertation or thesis or develop your skills base. Universities and colleges are developing a more sophisticated approach to the area of transferable skills (that is, those skills that will help you in your development as an academic and in your future career) and modules dealing with this subject can be taught with a minimal number of lectures. As a postgraduate, you will be expected to access these web pages as your course progresses.

How to make the most of it

- Firstly, do not panic! People love to use terms that seem to have been invented just to confuse you: e-learning, e-tutorials, electronic educational interface, web lectures, designated research databases and so on. In fact, all the electronic resources that support e-learning in all its forms should have been created to give you, the user, a minimal level of technological hassle. They should be easy to access, simple to understand and user-friendly at all stages. If you are uncomfortable with technology, do not to let your anxiety get in the way and at least try out the system that is in place for you: you may be pleasantly surprised.
- Get into the habit of asking about the IT backup that is available on each element of your course. Lecturers do not always remember to publicise these resources, so be persistent.
- If a site seems to be of little value to you at the beginning of your course, do not discard it forever. Revisit the site every few months to see if it has been updated or if its contents are now more relevant to you.
- Do not underestimate the value of study chat rooms. These might be set up under the website for one module of your course or might be more general in nature. Your lecturers might be available online for certain hours each week. You might discover a site specifically set up to support a series of presentations or placements that students are to undertake, to allow them to help each other as they face these challenges.
- Spend some time just browsing through what is available, although limit your browsing time to just a few hours, or a whole day might go by with very little being achieved. By browsing in this way you will be open to new possibilities. You might see study sites that are only loosely connected to your course, details of speakers and lecturers in whose work you have an interest or study skill sites that can support you.
- Be specific once you have browsed. The value of e-learning is reduced if you spend all your time just wandering. For most of your e-learning time you will need to be clear about what you want to get out of the system and avoid being led astray by other possible avenues. I recently taught a postgraduate who had decided, in his enthusiasm, to download an entire module onto hard copy so that he could work through it offline. His enthusiasm was seriously dented when he found that this relatively minor module on his course actually took up over 600 pages! He had spent so

long trying to wade through the entire site that he had no time or energy to carry out the tasks necessary to complete the module.

* Do not assume that the presence of e-learning material negates the need for real people. If you are unsure about some part of the course on a website, or feel that the chat room advice from other students is unreliable in your case, talk directly to a tutor. This can be done by email, of course, but you do not have to feel constrained by the technology. However technologically advanced we become, lecturers and tutors do still want to talk to their postgraduates and that is unlikely ever to change.

▶ Placements

What is involved

Placements on offer to postgraduates differ widely depending upon subject and course structure. A placement might be a year studying aboard, a term's industrial experience or just a few weeks within another university or professional setting. Although their format ranges widely (and they are not always a compulsory part of the course on which they feature), if a placement is made available to you, it is worth giving it serious consideration. There are, of course, advantages and disadvantages to this type of studying opportunity. The advantages might potentially include being able to escape the confines of your chosen institution, experience a wider range of research approaches and gain access to primary material that is available in a collection outside your institution. If you are a science or technology postgraduate, an industrial placement might be a vital tool in your endeavour to break into or develop your chosen career. The potential disadvantages of placements include the cost of travel and, possibly, accommodation (if this is not sufficiently funded by your university or college), the isolation that postgraduates can feel once away from their home institution and the logistics of fitting your placement experience into your overall research and working structure.

It is not always clear to postgraduates that a placement might be open to them. If it is not a compulsory element in your course, you could usefully spend some time considering whether a placement might be of value to you. Is there a collection of primary material elsewhere to which you need prolonged access? Would your statistical research be better carried out in a commerical setting? Is there a vocational placement that you have heard of that you feel would substantially boost your future career development? This is not a simple situation. Your university or college is unlikely to permit you to arrange a placement simply because it appeals to you, and competition for existing placements can be rigorous. Your decision as to whether to take up a placement or not will depend upon your individual circumstances, and any avenue that you pursue must be sanctioned at all stages by your supervisor, but there are several general points to bear in mind if you do undertake a placement.

How to make the most of them

- Find out everything that you can about your placement. You will not have to rely only upon the written information that you are given: talk to other postgraduates who have been on a placement already and make sure that you know who is arranging the placements so that you can approach them with your list of questions.
- Even if a placement is a compulsory part of your course, avoid leaving it to the last minute to get hold of as many details about it as you can. Lecturers and departmental secretaries will be happy to talk to you about what is involved, but may be pressed for time if you leave your questions until the week before you have to commit yourself to one particular placement.
- Placements are often allocated on a 'first come, first served' basis, so make sure that you are one of the first on the list. Although the details of a selection of placements will probably be posted up on a notice board, there may be other placements available, and it is frustrating to find out, too late, that the perfect one for you has now been allocated to another student.
- Put your support network in place well before you begin the placement. In a lengthy placement there will already be an established structure in place. In shorter placements you will still be allocated to a mentor and the staff at your university (particularly if you have a business liaison officer) will be on hand to help, but if the placement is carried out in a vacation, or if you are hesitant about contacting the university with what might seem to you to be a minor query, try to team up with another student who you can call, even if just for a chat and some moral support during your time away from university. Never suffer in silence if things begin to go wrong; there will always be someone available to help you.
- Once you have arranged to go on the placement that suits you, and are clear about what is expected of you, make sure that you comply with the requirements of the placement exactly. A placement might become a vitally important part of your postgraduate experience, even if you had not initially expected to be involved in such a scheme. The best way forward is to be absolutely sure about what is expected of you and make

the most of all the support that is available to you. As with so much else, communication is the key.

▶ Work-based projects

What is involved
As with placements, these vary widely from course to course. If you are on a vocational course, you might be expected to draw upon data from a commerical field. If you are undertaking a vocational distance learning course whilst working, most aspects of your professional life might in effect become a work-based project. The problem for postgraduates can be that of striking the balance between professional life and academic work, not just in terms of timing but also with reference to academic output. Time management will be discussed in Chapter 6, but guidelines will be offered here for getting the balance right and ensuring that the professional aspect of your life supports your academic work and vice versa.

How to make the most of them

- Make sure that everyone with whom you work is clear about the nature of the course that you are pursuing. They might not always be sympathetic, but it will allow you to be firm about the space you need to succeed in your postgraduate course if your colleagues are aware of the situation.
- Understand how your postgraduate work will support your professional development. Not every aspect of your course will be perfectly relevant to your work, but that is the pleasure of working as a postgraduate: it opens your eyes to new ways of working and the bigger issues that exist in your field of expertise. However, it is demoralising to lose your sense of purpose if your academic work seems to be diverging too far or for too long from your professional needs. Equally, if you are on an industrial placement, you need to be clear in advance that the project you are to complete will be relevant to your needs as an academic.
- Try to differentiate between purely academic work and applied professional expertise. Although you might be tempted to produce anecdotal evidence to support every point you make in a seminar, this will not necessarily help you to move forwards: you will need to develop a level of academic rigour that requires you to question your assumptions and contextualise your experiences. Similarly, you might feel inclined to discard your professional experience as 'not academic' enough for your current studying, whereas in fact your success will rely upon a blending of the

two. This is perhaps the biggest problem that professionals face in formalising their experiences within an academic setting; if you feel that this will be an issue for you, discuss it with your supervisor in the early stages of your course.

• If your professional activities are to be assessed as part of your course, make sure that you are in no doubt as to what is and is not being assessed. You will also need to be clear about who is to assess you. Will a professional mentor be involved or will the assessment be undertaken by your supervisor alone? This point should be made clear to you at the outset, but if you are in any doubt, get clarification before it becomes a worry to you. In this way, you will be able to ensure that your work-based experience is an integral and positive element in your postgraduate course.

Spot guide

Key points to remember from this chapter:

• attend every seminar that is open to you and be prepared to contribute
• lectures are opportunities to meet academics and see the wider implications of your subject
• visiting speakers and guest lecturers will expect you to get involved
• aim to go to several academic conferences so as to widen your horizons
• if there is no discussion group in your department, start one yourself
• tutorials are not to be feared, they are to be exploited
• e-learning is on the increase: you can make the most of it
• placements are not restricted to undergraduates: consider whether you could benefit
• work-based projects need time and care and can bring coherence to your vocational course

4 Your Skills Base

Troubleshooting guide

Read this chapter for help in the following areas:

- if you have not yet thought about your unique set of skills
- if you need help to identify your transferable skills
- if you want to read more productively
- if you are aiming to improve the ways in which you articulate your ideas
- if you feel that you could improve on your written presentation
- if you are worried about giving a presentation
- if you are unsure about your ability to solve problems logically
- if you would like to think more widely, laterally or creatively
- if you have trouble planning your work effectively
- if you would benefit from creating a skills inventory
- if you would like to work on your skills development plan
- if you have reached a sticking point in your research plan
- if you are not sure about the skills you can acquire as a postgraduate

There is now a growing emphasis upon the need for postgraduates to develop a credible 'transferable skills portfolio' during their time at university, which can be a rather unexpected element of your course. The anxiety felt by some postgraduates about this subject is partly due to the jargon attached to the process of acquiring these skills: 'experiential learning process', 'reflective action planning', 'career skills management' and so on. Once you get beyond the jargon, there are at least two good reasons for paying attention to this aspect of your postgraduate experience. The first is that you will have to employ a variety of differing skills in order to succeed in managing your course, so it is worth ensuring that you hone those skills as you progress so as to make this process easier. The second is that employers are looking for postgraduates who are able to demonstrate these skills (hence the term 'transferable skills', that is, those that transfer well into other areas of activity such as employment). This is one development that is driving universities, who are keen to see their postgraduates employed. The good news is that you should not have to do vast amounts of extra work in order to develop an impressive and, as importantly, effective skills base. It is much more a case of formalising and assessing the skills which you already have and then finding ways within your course to develop these in a positive and coherent way.

▶ Your range of skills

You will already have a wide range of skills that you use without consciously considering them and these will form the basis of your academic development. If you consider your everyday activities, you will soon begin to realise that you are employing most, if not all, of the following key skills on a regular basis:

- reading productively
- articulating your ideas
- reporting your results in writing
- writing persuasively
- presenting your work orally
- problem-solving
- thinking creatively
- planning effectively.

As soon as you read this list, you will probably be reminded of a job application or CV; these are the types of skills that employers love. Your instinct might be to turn away from such thoughts ('I have only just begun my course, I have no intention of thinking about a job yet') and this is understandable: of course you want to focus on your studying and research and enjoy it whilst you can. However, if you take another look at the list, it will be clear to you that these are also the skills you need in order to make a success of your course, so they are worth developing now. There are other skills that you will develop naturally as you progress: team working, managing your time, adapting your writing, coping with change, making informed and relevant connections within your research and managing your resources; these will all be discussed in the later chapters of this book. You will no doubt be able to extend this list, as each postgraduate course offers a differing range of opportunities for skills development.

Before moving on to look at the skills listed above in more depth, a brief word on the subject of employers. They need skilled employees, but they also want you to show that you have the personal qualities that can arise from such a skills base. They will be attracted by a postgraduate who will fit into their team and whose personal qualities will complement their organisation and its aims. Breaking into a new career will be the focus of Chapter 11, but you can see from the list of personal qualities below (all of which can develop naturally from the skills itemised above) how you might become an attractive potential colleague for any employer simply by assessing and using your skills base:

- determination
- the will to succeed
- flexibility
- curiosity
- the ability to cope with change
- self-discipline
- analytical proficiency
- self-motivation
- thinking clearly
- expressing yourself thoughtfully
- applying common sense to challenges.

You will already possess many of these qualities and have begun to develop some of these skills before your current course. The task ahead of you now is to analyse how your skills base might be utilised and developed.

▶ Postgraduate skills development

By analysing the skill areas that I have identified, you will be in a position to make the move forward in developing a credible skills base. This is an intrinsic part of the self-management mentioned at the outset of this book. The ways in which you can use and develop your skills in each of these key areas are discussed below.

▶ Reading productively

Reading effectively for research and reading backup material to support that research are both vital skills that you will need to develop and they are therefore explored extensively in this book. In Chapter 6 the skills required to manage research resources (primary material, manuscript sources, court records, statistics and the like) are discussed. Here the focus is upon secondary sources: the books that you will read not because they are essential primary material, but because you will have to read widely in order to contextualise your primary research.

You may be given a series of reading lists, or perhaps a list of suggested reading that you have developed from talking around your subject in seminars and tutorials. You will want to add to these the books and journals mentioned in any lectures you attend. Undergraduates can often find themselves overwhelmed with huge departmental reading lists that they find difficult to handle; you may feel some initial relief that this has not happened to you as a postgraduate, but you will have to create far longer personalised reading lists that can become just as daunting as anything faced by an undergraduate. Take the example of one book or journal that you find useful. You feel that the author had really grasped this aspect of your subject and so you take copious notes and are inspired to read more. You turn to the bibliography or 'suggested reading' pages of the publication, only to find that there are perhaps twenty or thirty books and articles listed (sometimes many more) and you have the task of wading through this list, trying to make sensible decisions about which books to read and which to discard. What is certain is that you cannot read them all, so you have to make a choice. How you make this choice will be explored in Chapter 6, but we can assume here that you have compiled a list of books that you feel would be useful to you.

Faced with your principal reading list, in your plans you might overlook that you also have other works to read: extracts or articles given to you in advance of seminars, conference proceedings, either on hard copy or the Internet, and, of course, your leisure reading. As you can see, the life of a postgraduate is made up in no small part of reading; not just reading, but also selecting, analysing, assimilating material and using it judiciously. You will already know about your preferred style of reading (slow and steady, fast and furious, patchy but productive), but life as a postgraduate will demand that you learn to skim read effectively, work steadily through some texts and read at speed whilst taking notes when the pressure is on. Taking notes is a skill you will already have mastered in your earlier studying, but it is worth mentioning here that notes you take from any situation, whether lectures and seminars, books or the Internet, must show clearly the distinction between your ideas and those taken from elsewhere. This habit must be rigorously adopted and absolutely unbreakable throughout your course. Plagiarism is a risk that is simply not worth taking; most postgraduates would be indignant at the very suggestion that they would do such a thing, but you can find yourself mistakenly quoting a source without realising it if you are not very careful to make your sources clear in every set of notes you make.

If you get into the habit of marking and naming your sources at every stage, you will protect yourself from this risk and the results of plagiarism, which are always severe within the academic community.

There are books available to help you to expand your range of reading skills, but the key to managing your reading is to recognise that, at any one time, you are likely to have up to five different sorts of reading material to hand, each sort making different demands upon your skills.

You might have *recommended, principal texts* with which you will become familiar over the course of your study, texts widely considered to be the seminal works of reference in your field. The secret with these is not to let them overwhelm you or feel that they represent the last word in an area of research. You will have to begin to read these texts in the first few weeks of your course and this should, of course, be done with some care, but you need not force yourself to understand every paragraph or pressurise yourself to grasp every concept in its entirety. It may take further independent research before you fully appreciate what is being said by an acknowledged expert in your field. You will be revisiting these books frequently, so you will be reading at each stage, knowing that you can handle them in manageable chunks as your understanding increases.

You will have *essential backup reading* to do in order to support your research and seminars. Your relationship with these texts might be short-lived, and they are often available on limited loan time in the library or, if they are articles from journals, within your own department. If you decide to develop specific seminar work within your own research, you may decide to buy some of these texts, but you will want to work with them for a time before deciding whether to invest in them as permanent resources. Initially, the reading skills involved in using them will be different from those demanded by the principal, set texts. You will be approaching these texts with your particular seminar and research requirements in mind and with an awareness of what is contained within your principal texts. You are much more likely, therefore, as you make notes on these books, to be arguing with some of the premises contained within them and comparing theories. In many ways this reading is much more active. You are not expected to soak up the book in its entirety, rather you are asked to use it as an aid to sharpen your reasoning skills and deepen your understanding.

You will be using some books as a very *immediate aid* in producing a specific piece of work. These books are often (and sometimes most usefully) collections of essays and you may well need them only in order to read one or two of the essays in the collection. Reading essay collections is the quickest way to assess whether you have covered all the varying aspects of a field of study: they are also a great way to familiarise yourself with the arguments that range around a subject, without you needing to examine every single facet of it yourself in depth. You are unlikely to read these books from cover to cover and you will be skim reading many of them; you might simply browse through the index in order to find the one or two references within the text that may be of use to you. These are also the books from which you are most likely to be photocopying sections or even single pages. It is far easier to attach a photocopied section to your own notes than to make extensive notes of your own, but there are two points to remember when you do this. Firstly, make sure that you make an exact and extensive note of the title, author and publication details of the book on your photocopy. Remember that you are going to be creating your own bibliography shortly and there is nothing more frustrating than wasting valuable time in the library hunting for a book to which you wish to refer, but the details of which you forgot to take at the time. It can also be disastrous, if you have photocopied a section of a book that is now out on loan for three months, or that only came to you in the first place via the interlibrary loan system.

Secondly, you need to make sure that you take ownership of the information contained within the photocopied section or chapter. It is a lovely feeling to have spent the morning in the library, photocopying all sorts of useful information, and then to put all the photocopies neatly into plastic wallets in your files. Sadly, you may then ignore them for weeks or even months and then realise that you have no idea, when you come to look at them, why you ever thought they were relevant, particularly if your research has taken a new turn since you first made the photocopies. You can also find that, because you have not highlighted the relevant sentences, you have to struggle through vast tracts of material before finding the one reference you need. So, you must decide in advance to divide your time equally between identifying and finding the books, photocopying the relevant sections and then having a cup of coffee whilst you highlight the sections or sentences that you will need for future reference. Then you can put them in plastic wallets in your files, with their full references noted down, and feel truly virtuous.

You will have books that you have set aside for *leisure reading*. These will include the latest thrillers or romantic novels, but you will also have books dealing with issues on the periphery of your course, texts that you will not expect to make extensive notes on but that will be useful to you in terms of giving you background information. If, for example, the title of your dissertation or thesis is to be 'The impact of World War II on social trends in postwar Manchester', it would be useful to read some war poetry, selected war diaries or the biographies of leading political and social figures. You will not make many notes on these texts: they are there to help you to immerse yourself in the atmosphere of the period you are studying. However, you will need to balance your leisure reading. If you know that you are the sort of reader who can never relax and so will leap up from your bed each night to make notes on the biography that is meant to be for leisure reading, or if you find that you will sleep badly if you read anything related to your course, then finish off with a good trashy novel each night, or allow yourself the time every now and then to read something in your leisure time that is entirely unrelated to your field.

The last set of books that might haunt your postgraduate days are those which you feel you *ought to read*, even though they are too dense for you to get to grips with or, as can happen, almost unreadable. It is easy to fall into the trap of thinking that, because you are a postgraduate, you really ought to be able to master every book that bears any relation to your subject area, yet this is simply not the case. Some authors write badly, whatever the subject, and thus the fact that you cannot get to grips with their work is their fault, not yours. Even with books written in an accessible style, you might be unable to master every concept or understand every viewpoint. Most post-graduates could tell you of the book that dogged them throughout their course, or the theory that they could not master, and the sense of awkwardness that this left them feeling. Of course, you will want to understand all the major theories in your field and make use of the concepts, ideas and viewpoints presented to you, but you are not a failure if a few stones are left unturned, and talking to your tutor about any insurmountable hurdles you encounter should put your mind at rest as to the relevance of the theory in question. The books you simply cannot master tend to gravitate towards the bottom of your reading pile, and the management technique to employ here is to make yourself have a good clear out of your book pile at the end of each term. If a book has been sitting, unread, on the pile, be honest with yourself. Are you ever going to read it? Is it essential to the development of your research? Is it enhancing your postgraduate experience? If the answer to all these questions is no (and it probably will be), be ruthless with your-self and return the book to the library. It will be available later if you suddenly need it, but at least it will not be in your sight all the time.

Once you have grasped that the huge pile of books loitering meaningfully in the corner of your room, or relentlessly weighing down your bags, can in fact be divided into these five categories, you will feel far more in control. You know that some of the books will be read in their entirety over the course of a few weeks or months, but you also have the consolation of knowing that most of them will be read only partially and in a very different style from the way in which you will approach your principal set of texts. Books viewed in this way become tools to be used in a variety of ways, not all of which are too time consuming. You will be able to use your differing reading skills, plan your reading schedule according to your mood, work commitments and energy levels and get on constructively with one of the most enjoyable activities of postgraduate life: reading.

▶ Articulating your ideas

As social beings we articulate our ideas every day without giving them much thought. We instinctively express each idea, from what we might eat for lunch to what we think about the current economic climate, in terms that suit the seriousness of the topic and the audience to which we are offering the idea. As a postgraduate, you will be faced with a new challenge: that of articulating academic ideas in a structured way and within what is a relatively formal environment. You will probably already have some experience of doing this, either in your undergraduate or professional life, but now the situation is more complex, the possibility for confusion or error greater. You are expected to develop your own theories, back these up with research and bring ideas and questions to each studying opportunity. Testing your ideas and articulating them with confidence and authority is going to be essential to your success in managing your postgraduate course, and it is an area that causes more anxiety for students than almost any other. You will need to get the balance right: not just relying on vague ideas or anecdotal evidence, but also not so weighed down with received theory that you are unable to express any ideas of your own.

The solution to the problem is learning to assess your ideas in a systematic way. There will be at least five different sorts of idea in your mind at any time during your course.

Building perhaps on your earlier studying and background reading, you will be gathering a set of *received ideas* within your field. These are the initial building blocks upon which you will develop your research. This set comprises some ideas that are so widely acknowledged as to be in the public domain. If, for example, your area of study is criminology, you need not cite backup material every time you wish to discuss the unreliability of eyewitness accounts, as this knowledge is widely held and understood. It also includes ideas that may not be public knowledge but are widely understood and accepted in your specialist field. In the given case of criminology, the idea that the reliability of eyewitness accounts decreases if the perpetrator of a crime was wearing the colour red is one such idea. You will assimilate these ideas with little conscious effort, but you do need to carry out a 'reliability check' on each section of your written work in the early checking stages. Are the ideas or facts that you have presented really taken as entirely watertight by the academic community? Do you need to cite precedents or present evidence to support your statements? Should you pick apart a received idea in order to gain some research leverage or should you accept it as a starting point?

One of the pleasures of postgraduate life is the opportunity it allows you to work with *discussion ideas*. These will not reflect your final thoughts on an area of your subject, and they can be articulated in three ways. You will be trying out ideas within your seminar group as you begin to form your own theories and explore your way forward within your research. You might produce discussion ideas at the end of an academic paper or a seminar presentation with the intention of getting everyone talking, and will not mind if your idea is dissected and discredited by the end of the session. You might, if you feel confident enough, ask questions at the end of a paper to which you have been listening, perhaps given by a guest speaker or your tutor, simply because you are unsure of the potential range of a field of study or are unclear about how it can be of value to you. The importance of discussion ideas will depend upon two factors. Firstly, you must be sure that you can differentiate between a considered idea, one that you have worked on and for which you have evidence, and a discusssion idea. Secondly, you must be brave. It can make you feel rather vulnerable just to toss an idea in the air and hope that someone picks up on it, but that is what seminars are for. If the idea is entirely without merit (and this is improbable), it will be dismissed within seconds, but if it gives grounds for discussion you will be thankful you raised it. Some of your most fruitful areas of research are likely to arise from discussion ideas, so they are worth pursuing.

You will also be grappling with your *initial research ideas* as you progress through your course. You might not discuss these with anyone for many weeks as you work out how they might be of value to you and how you can develop them. They often arise from the marginal notes you have made during seminars or whilst talking with your supervisor, or they might be ideas in which you have always believed but which you now want to test. They can niggle at you for months before you feel in a position to explore them further or they might be very much in the back of your mind until a new area of research reminds you of them. You will inevitably disregard some of these ideas in the end; indeed, you might cringe when you think of them once you have mastered your subject more fully. However, these ideas should be treated with respect: they are a sign that you are developing as an academic in your own right. They will provide you with many of the most inspirational points in your journey through your subject and they will enliven and inform your research, which is as much about asking questions as it is about finding answers.

Your academic output (your thesis or dissertation, your coursework and any articles or academic papers you produce) will be made up of *developed ideas*, those ideas you have worked through and subjected to rigorous academic thought and evidential testing. You will be relieved to know that this does not mean that every idea you include in your work must be absolutely without the possibility of refutation by others: academic life thrives on the proposing and subsequent testing of ideas. However, you must be able to distinguish between developed and undeveloped ideas. You might, for example, choose to conclude each section of your dissertation or thesis with a set of ideas which you feel are raised by the issues you have covered; this is a valid technique as long as your reader knows that you are not claiming these as any more than starting points for future research. The danger really arises when you become so single-minded about an idea – it must be right and evidence must exist to support it somewhere – that you cannot resist including it, dressing it up in language which suggests that it is a developed rather than an undeveloped idea. For example, a postgraduate studying demographic trends in England in the seventeenth century might be struck by the high rate of infant mortality and the lack of elaborate funeral rites for these infants. It is a small but dangerous step to assume it to be self-evident that such deaths were therefore thought to be of little consequence in that period, with inadequate reference to supporting evidence. If this claim is then put forward as a developed idea, it will sit there just waiting for a social historian to discredit it by reference to diaries and letters of the period.

You are interested in your field of study and committed to exploiting every scrap of knowledge that you possess, and therefore you will be besieged by *irrelevant ideas*, which can be both demoralising and disconcerting. In reality, the fact that some of your ideas will be irrelevant to your work should be taken as a good sign. It does not mean that the ideas are in themselves worthless, it simply means that they will not add substantially to the body of your work at this stage. They demonstrate that you are thinking creatively and laterally about your subject, so they should be welcomed as indicators of your lively intelligence, rather than being viewed as embarrassing dead ends in your intellectual development. Irrelevant ideas are not going to be a problem to you as long as you can spot them and not let them distract you. You will soon get into the habit of discarding such ideas as soon as they arise. For example, you are searching the Internet for background information on an essay concerning the development of genetic engineering in the American farming community. You will no doubt be fascinated as you notice other stray facts, all of which might spark off irrelevant ideas. The plight of farmers in Zimbabwe might be helped or hindered by genetic engineering, possibly you should have chosen that as your subject? The depression caused widespread hardship in America, perhaps that led to economic reforms? The potato famine in Ireland resulted in mass emigration to America, maybe that will have had a long-term impact upon attitudes towards agricultural production in both countries? All these questions are interesting, but they might all be irrelevant to the project you have in hand. You will need to note them (if nothing else, this will get them out of your system and allow you to focus on your research task) and work through them later, perhaps, if you find you need more ideas in developing your work.

The insidious problem you might face in weeding out irrelevant ideas, particularly in the first stages of your course, is twofold. You are naturally reluctant to discard any ideas, just in case you need them. This problem eases as you develop more ideas: each one seems slightly less precious in itself unless it supports your existing line of argument or takes you onto a new track that you really believe will be productive. You are also now exploring a new language, some words of which might be familiar to you, but some of which might glamorise ideas you would otherwise discard instantly. If, for example, you are studying psychology, you will soon discover that REM is no longer a rock band to you, but the abbreviation for rapid eye movement. This new language is exciting, it allows you to articulate your ideas more fully, but it can also distort your perception of the importance of your ideas. Again, this problem eases with experience. You will become so used to the language of your field that it ceases to impress you and you will then be able to revisit your earliest ideas in order to assess their importance in the light of your subsequent research.

▶ Reporting your results in writing

The more sophisticated writing techniques that you will develop as a postgraduate will be discussed in Chapter 9, but you will probably be asked to express your ideas in writing within just a few weeks of beginning your course, perhaps far earlier than you feel ready to do this. There are several ways to tackle this challenge.

Look at *precedent*. If you are asked to produce a short paper for your seminar group and you are not sure how it should be laid out, what proportion of the paper should be factual and how much speculation, how far you should be seeking to raise questions and how far to answer them, do not be afraid to ask your tutor whether you can take a brief look at a similar paper produced by a former student, just so that you can get an idea of the most appropriate layout and level of the contents.

Get clear *guidelines*. Even if your department or school does not issue a set of guidelines for each piece of writing you might be asked to produce, your tutor should be able to advise you. You need to ask: what is the word count? Are there penalties for exceeding this or is it just a guide? Is the work to be in report or essay format? Will you be expected to include footnotes and a bibliography?

If you are unsure of your ability to write effectively, you might work through some of the suggestions in Chapter 9, but it is also a good idea to book onto a *study skills course* as early as you can. These courses are designed to support you in specific areas of your academic life, and attending writing workshops and seminars will increase your confidence and help you to master any aspects of academic writing with which you are unfamiliar, as well as guiding you through the eccentricities of spelling, punctuation and grammar. If you leave it until later, you will be under pressure to produce more complex pieces of writing and might lack the time to get to grips with the basics.

One of the surest ways to increase your writing skills base is to *archive your work*. Keep a hard copy of each piece of written work you produce during your course (this is usually more effective that relying on electronic copies, unless you are very adept at revising and analysing work on your computer screen). These copies will be invaluable to you. They will allow you to analyse your previous writing skills in order to assess your progress, remind you of what worked well in terms of layout and ordering when you come to produce more work and give you some core material that you can revisit and, if possible, adapt and reuse in future pieces of writing.

▶ Writing persuasively

The art of writing persuasively is, for many postgraduates, a natural development from the fundamental skills of writing accurately and in an academic style. Remember that, whatever you write, you will always be trying to persuade somebody of something, whether it is simply persuading them to agree with a particular argument or, in the final stages of your course, persuading an examiner that you are worthy of the qualification for which you are aiming. If you feel that there is still work to be done on your style in order to make it more persuasive, you do not need to wait until you are well advanced in your course; there are some points that you could consider straight away.

Who are your readers? This may seem like a simplistic question, but it is surprising how often writers, even experienced academic writers, forget to think of their readers. The writing process becomes all about you, what you want to say, what you know about a subject, and far too little about the readers, what they are expecting, what they want to know, how they might be persuaded. The plural term 'readers' is used here advisedly, as academic writing tends to reach a wide readership and you need to be aware of this. Even a simple résumé of your research activities might be lodged with your supervisor, only to be distributed far more widely than you had expected, as research panels or the head of your department or school take an interest in your work. Other researchers, too, with your permission, might be shown the résumé if they have a related field of interest. More formal pieces of writing, such as journal articles or conference papers, will reach a much wider readership and it is vital that you do all the necessary research on that readership. Is the journal highly specialised, appealing only to a narrow field of readers, or is it more general in nature? Will your conference paper be heard only on that occasion or will it be distributed via the Internet or perhaps even published, in which case you will be seeking to persuade a far more general readership of your viewpoint and academic prowess?

How formal should you be? Should you be highly formal in all that you write, incurring the risk that you might appear pompous or unwilling to accept advice and ideas? Or should you be a little less formal, with the danger that you might appear too casual, not rigorous enough in your standards and academic vetting? Again, experience and research are the solutions to this problem. You will get to know the tone that will suit each piece of writing and there should be clear departmental guidelines to help you. At the very least, you need to ensure that you are aware of your readers and can make a reasonable judgement about the level of formality they will expect, but do not become too concerned about this unless you have been told by your lecturers that it is a problem you need to address.

How will you persuade? Obviously you will persuade by the force of your argument, the quality of your evidence and the passion for your subject that is shown in your writing, but beyond this there are simple techniques you can employ. Their usefulness will vary depending upon the writing you are producing, but in every case you will need to allow your reader plenty of space to 'breathe' whilst reading, so wide margins, double spacing and a roomy layout are essential. Readers need the 'white space' of breaks within the text in order to feel comfortable as they progress. You should also avoid jargon, unless you are absolutely sure that your reader will be familiar with the terms you are using. You will 'signpost' your writing, making it clear to the reader that there is a logical order to your arguments and the reader will be led through it without any unwelcome surprises. This might be done by including lists to show the points you intend to cover, inserting a sentence or two at the end of a section in which you recap very briefly on what you have just written and ensuring that each new section of writing begins with a clear statement of what you intend to cover next. Finally, you need to get into the habit of 'listening' to your writing. Initially, this might mean going back to a piece of writing that you produced some time ago and reading it aloud. You might feel a little awkward doing this at first, but it does produce results. As you read a section of writing, imagine that you are on stage, reading it aloud to a large audience. Slightly exaggerate the pauses, put some dramatic impact into what you are saying. You will be surprised at the results: suddenly your writing is no longer in your head, it is out in the open and far more reminiscent of how it will be received by a reader than how it appeared in your mind as you wrote it. As you read, ask yourself questions: does it sound strained or pompous? Are you bullying the readers into agreeing with you or leading them along a path with you? Are your sentences overly long or rambling or are they too note-like in form? Do you sound confident or weak? Do your sentences keep the reader engaged? Does your paragraph structure allow the reader to 'escape' for a moment or two in order to consider what you are saying? Once you have developed the habit of reading aloud like this, you will find that you can read your writing on the page with a voice inside your head, as if you were reading it aloud, and you can pinpoint problems and overcome difficulties easily.

▶ Presenting your work orally

Presentations will form part of the disucsssion in Chapter 9, but there is work you can do to manage your oral presentation skills from the first few weeks of your course. If you know that you are likely to encounter problems with presentations, try one of these approaches now.

Assess your *presentation experience*. Can you increase your confidence by thinking back to a time when you had to give a presentation, even in a relatively informal way, to a small audience? If you can, then you are in a position to analyse the experience. What went well? What went less well? Where did your strengths lie? What comments did you receive after the presentation and can these be used to guide you now? For informal situations in which you will be asked to present your ideas orally, such as seminars, group discussions, guest speaker papers, supervisions and tutorials, you will still be able to draw on your past experience by considering how you react in meetings (Do you chair them? Do you contribute well? Do you find it difficult to speak up?) or social groups (Are you quieter than most of your friends? Do you lead the group?). This analysis of your experience will help you to assess whether you are likely to face problems in presenting your academic work orally.

If you are still uncertain about your skills in this area, there are *analytical tests* that you can undertake. These can reveal whether you are naturally a chairperson or a team player, an innovator or a consolidator; they can also reveal your personality type and preferences. Such tests might be available from your university's Careers Advisory Service. They will not necessarily solve any problem that you might encounter, of course, but they will help you to analyse your starting position with regard to the challenge of oral presentations.

As with so many aspects of life, *practice makes perfect* in presentations. It may be a cliché, but it is true nevertheless. Postgraduates on presentation skill courses are regularly amazed at how swiftly they can improve on their base skills in this area, sometimes with very little specialist help. With even the most minimal level of help and support, you will find that practice is the secret of success. If you are not convinced, try giving a small presentation at home, perhaps just for five minutes or so. Make yourself practise it at least six times, leaving a short gap between each practice. You will find that you are almost unrecognisably better, clearer, more measured and far more confident by the end of an hour.

▶ Problem-solving

It is all too easy to spend much of your time as a postgraduate effectively reinventing the wheel in terms of your research skills. Although Chapter 6 will cover research techniques and strategies extensively, for the development of your overall skills base you need to capture these research skills, analyse and assess them and then adapt or develop them as you progress. Let us take, for example, a postgraduate science student who is attempting to prove a scientific theory. The student spends time studying scientific literature to see how an existing theory could be extended or trying to develop a new theory. More time is then spent developing a computer modelling system or setting up a laboratory experiment as part of the process of proving the theory. Once this has been completed, more effort is required to write up the results, contextualising them within the existing body of scientific knowledge and trying to extrapolate the original hypothesis in the light of the results. This procedure is core to the postgraduate experience of that student and will form the basis of the academic work that arises from it, but what may be overlooked are the general applications that can be drawn from the process. When, a year later, the student needs to test and evaluate another theory, there is a danger of beginning the process from scratch rather than exploiting this previous experience. In order to avoid this pitfall, you need to develop a system of capturing your research experience.

In everything that you do, try to *separate the particular from the general*. If, for example, you have found a statistical analysis process that works well with samples of over 1,000 statistical subjects, analyse why it works and make a note of this at the time. You may not have to handle such a large sample group for many months, but your notes will be there to refresh your mind when you are faced with a similar situation again. This technique also has the benefit of ensuring that you are not wasting your time, even if one research task turns out to be of limited immediate help to you. So, for example, if you find an especially interesting and useful CD-ROM that is not relevant to your research now, store the information so that you can come back to it if you need to in the future. In this particular instance, it is of little help to you but its general value may be enormous. Similarly, if you find that writing research questions on index cards helps you to organise a particularly thorny area of your research, be ready to employ the technique in the future.

When you are working your way through textbooks, see them as *templates for research*. Take note not just of the material that is being presented to you, but notice also the ways in which it has been ordered so as to make it accessible. Does the writer use graphs and charts more than is usual? Are there bullet point lists to help you to grasp the main points? Does each section end in a summary? Is chronological information reordered so as to enhance specific themes? This may seem to be an issue of effective reading and writing, but actually you can employ similar techniques in your own research notes, so that you can improve their accessibility and order your own thoughts.

You will be growing as an academic until the moment you submit your final coursework, dissertation or thesis. For this reason you must see each new occasion as a *research lesson*. Rather than simply listening to papers by other academics, ask them how they tackled the big research issues which they faced, how they order their material within their research tasks and how they go about testing each new hypothesis. In a seminar or discussion group you will naturally be receptive to other people's ideas, but trying to get behind these ideas to discover the means by which they arrived at them can sometimes be of greater value to you than the ideas themselves. Your research skills base will need to be continually monitored, updated and reviewed if you are to make the most of it.

▶ Thinking creatively

Being able to think creatively is one of the greatest challenges and most satisfying achievements of being a postgraduate. You might have to think laterally if you find yourself at a dead end or think around a subject if your original hypothesis appears to be breaking down. You will be expected to think as widely as possible in order to test and contextualise your work and yet you will also be asked to think through the minutiae of each situation so that the details fit into place. Some of this will come easily to you, and you are likely to be the sort of person who either thinks widely or likes to give attention to details, but whichever category you fall into, there are ways of ensuring that your skills base is as wide and productive as possible.

If you find yourself at a dead end, try *brainstorming*. This technique can be adapted to differing situations, but in this context it would involve taking a large, blank sheet of paper, letting your mind wander around the difficulty, keeping your central topic in 'soft focus' mentally and jotting down thoughts that crop up all over the paper. This often works well if you can persuade a group of friends to work on it with you. The thoughts do not have to be well focused, nor do they have to be directly relevant to the central problem, so friends who are not experts in your area can join in, and it is often a stray thought from a non-expert that will fire you up again. By the end of the session you will be left with a rather messy piece of paper, but do not try to make any sense of it straightaway. Leave it for 24 hours and then come back to it afresh, in a more structured frame of mind. Take each point on the page and think through whether it can be of use to you, perhaps by extending your current thinking in an existing area of research or by showing you a quite different way forward. It is often the case that the most far-flung thoughts are of the greatest benefit in transporting you out of your dead end. Once you have set off on your new track, keep the brainstorming results for future reference, just in case you get stuck again and do not have the time, or the inclination, to throw another brainstorming party.

Every now and then (perhaps every week when you are in the midst of writing up a piece of research), carry out a *focus review*. This is not an onerous task and need not take up much of your time. As you work your way through your course, you will be offered new ideas, shown new ways of looking at old issues and challenged to test and reassess your theories. This is exciting and will help you to reach new areas of thought, but it can also misdirect you. If, for example, you were intending to focus in a major piece of research on the persecution of witches in early modern America, you would be keen to master all the relevant information, but you would also encounter supporting material that must be handled carefully. In this example, you would explore the political situation that led to the persecution, the view of women that could have allowed such a thing to happen, the development of medicine, the role of the church and the activities of prophetesses and female poets. You might find all this fascinating, but you need to ensure that you do not become engrossed in peripheral aspects of your subject to the detriment of your central hypothesis. Of course, you might undertake a focus review and decide to treat your subject quite differently, or branch out into a new area and drop another, and this need not be a problem, as long as you are aware of, and truly happy with, your new focus. As already mentioned, however many words you are allocated, you will find them insufficient for what you would like to say, but checking periodically that you are still focused on your main theme will help you to use your time and word count to best effect.

Along with your periodic focus review, you will need to carry out a *details check* on a regular basis, perhaps once a fortnight. This may sound boring, but in fact it is a satisfying and confidence-boosting task. Think of it as an academic spring clean. You will have notes, lists of references to check and texts to look up, as well as half-completed pieces of work. To carry out a details check you simply work through your notes: are they in order? Is there any information that should be transferred to your reading list? Have you followed up on any ideas that are written in the margin? You then turn to your lists of references: do you need to order more books? Are you really happy about missing out that detailed quote or piece of data simply because you will have to spend an hour hunting for it? Do you need to email a colleague to get a more accurate reference for a passing comment made in a seminar? Your draft work in progress will also need a spring clean: have you made claims which really require some expansion to make your meaning clear? Have you made assumptions without bothering to back them up with evidence? Has your writing become too generalised, when a few detailed examples would make it more effective and persuasive? This is a pleasant task to do at the end of a busy week, but try not to be led astray into carrying out a whole series of revisions: this is not the moment to rush off and find the missing books or revise a whole section of your work, it is simply an opportunity for you to make a list of what you need to do next and make sure that all your various reading lists are up to date. You are not forcing yourself to be creative or necessarily to think great new thoughts, but instead you will feel by the end of the details check that everything is in the right place and your research is as watertight as it can be at this stage.

Writing up an extensive piece of research, either for an essay, a report or a lengthier piece of writing, can become a very introspective experience and an *outsider's check* will become essential. You will be enjoying the work (for most of the time!) but you might also start to feel as if you are working in ever-decreasing circles, developing tunnel vision and losing the thread of the bigger picture. The cure for this is simple: just ask a friend or colleague to take a look at what you have produced. This will work well if you can arrange to review regularly the work of colleagues in exchange for similar help from them. If you can, avoid relying on just one colleague for this help, as you might not increase your field of vision widely enough in this way. Instead, develop a network of friends and colleagues whose help you can call upon when you begin to feel that a fresh perspective on your work is needed. This is, of course, in addition to your supervisions, which will serve a similar purpose.

Whether you are engrossed in a complex section of your research or embroiled in a challenging piece of writing, you will need some *space to think*. It sounds obvious: you are, after all, thinking about your subject for much of the time. However, you still need some unstructured thinking space, some time when you can think around your subject in a loose way, trying to get the overall shape of your research in your mind (it will be changing all the time) and hoping for a flash of inspiration as to where you might go next. To some extent, the formal elements of your course, seminars, lectures and discussion groups, will provide this space. They will lift you out of your introspection for a short time and allow you to think about other areas of your subject, and if they do not hold your attention entirely that will also allow your mind to wander a little in a structured way. However, you need space beyond this if you are to give yourself a chance to reassess your work and assimilate some of the wider implications of what you have discovered. Regardless of the level of pressure on you, you will always benefit from a break that allows you to think. If you take a walk or a weekend off, you might feel guilty, but deciding in advance exactly when you will return to work will ease that feeling and you will be thinking on some level about your work, so you will know that you are still moving forward.

A postgraduate course is a cumulative process and for this reason you will need to *revisit the past* occasionally. Never see any work as complete: even the most basic of your early essays might be of value to you in the future. If you have given a seminar presentation, you might leave it to one side for a time and then use it as a springboard to new ways of approaching your subject in the future. A research review, produced for your supervisor, might be written with concern only to get everything down on paper ready for your supervision, but revisiting it several months later will remind you of where you were then, and allow you to make sure that you have not left any research loose ends dangling. There is another great advantage to this process: it will give you the satisfaction of knowing that you have progressed substantially in your work and with this comes an increase in your confidence as an academic.

▶ Planning effectively

Whatever you are producing as a postgraduate, from a minor essay to a major thesis, you can only work at your best if you *plan everything*. This may be a new concept for you: perhaps you are not a natural planner and tend to rely more on inspiration at the time, or the pressure of a deadline, in order to get through your work. This approach is unlikely to work once you are studying at postgraduate level. This is partly a matter of practicalities: if you plan your work, you can time your workload, discuss your plans with your supervisor and feel secure in how your work is developing. It is also a matter of confidence. Postgraduates often express concern about the minutiae of their work: is my grammar and spelling up to scratch? Why does this hypothesis feel rather strained? Why does that paragraph sound weak? In reality, their problems are actually being caused by poor planning. They are confused about the overall shape of a piece of work, so the execution of it on paper comes across in a more confused way. They know roughly what they want to say, but it sounds weak or unsupported because they have not planned how to test a hypothesis rigorously as they progress. Once you feel secure in your plan, knowing exactly where you are going and how you intend to get there, you will have the confidence to commit yourself to paper and the time and space to pay attention to the details as you do this.

If you are to plan everything, you will need to know about *your preferred planning method*. In Chapter 9 there is an extensive discussion of planning methods, and this will help you to decide on which method, or methods, will work for you. Your preferred method will not work for everything you do, but you will at least feel comfortable with the way in which you are working in most cases. Trying to apply a planning method that does not suit you can be very confusing. The shape of the work you are planning just will not become clear and you feel that your preparation is inadequate: in fact, it is more likely that you need to try out another planning method on the task in hand.

Although you will come to enjoy the structure that good planning can offer you, you must remain *flexible in your planning*. Plans should not be strait-jackets, constraining your thoughts and controlling every word you write. Instead they should be enablers, keeping you on track as you move ahead, but open to adaptation and revision periodically. Once you have a plan in place, use it as you begin your writing, presentation preparation or research task, but revise it regularly.

As with so much else in the management of a postgraduate course, *preparation is the key*. Your planning will extend beyond simply the production of written work. It will be vital to the management of all your research activities, indeed, you will be planning your whole course. Undergraduates can expect to have some of their work planned for them: they will have rigid deadlines, frequent seminars and lectures and regular tutorials. Postgraduates plan for themselves, with the support of a supervisor, and this is one of the most important aspects of managing your course.

▶ Analysing and developing your skills base

Developing your skills base is not something that you can easily do towards the end of your course. You need to start work on it early if it is to be really productive and become part of the management of your postgraduate career. It will not be necessary to undertake huge amounts of additional work in order to develop your skills base in an organised and effective way; it is more a case of formalising what you know about yourself already and planning how you might maximise the opportunities that will come your way.

The easiest way to achieve this is to work out a skills inventory for yourself. This involves identifying the skills you will need on your course and, as importantly, those which will be useful to you in your future life and career. You will then be in a position to analyse the ways in which your current activities might enhance those skills and set yourself challenges in your own developmental journey as you reassess periodically how far you have travelled. Producing a skills inventory in a formal way might seem like yet another piece of work in an already overcrowded life, but it brings with it so many benefits that once you have begun, you will enjoy the process.

Let us take as an example an English postgraduate who is undertaking a one-year masters course, with a view to continuing on to a three-year PhD if things go well. She took a break of several years after gaining her degree and worked in a marketing company. She likes to be in control of life, so she tends to plan essays very tightly and suspects that she will overplan her whole course. She has had little experience in giving formal presentations and was horrified to find that presentations are to form part of her assessment. She might have many skills areas that need developing, but for the purposes of this example we will assume that she is three months into her course and has been focusing on four of the key skills discussed in this chapter. She will produce a skills portfolio when she comes to produce a CV, having read Chapter 11 of this book, but for now she needs a working document that can be revised and developed as she progresses. It will look something like this.

Planning	
Why do I need it?	• need to let my research develop
	• need to be open to new ideas
	• need to keep my course under control
Review skill experience	• how did I plan the charity campaign at work?
	• what works well for me in time management?
How can I develop it?	• work through this term planning each week's work
	• revise the plan each month
	• decide on my best planning method
	• work with my supervisor to plan my dissertation

- always revise essay plans as I write them

Where do I go next?

Thinking creatively

Why do I need it?
- to broaden my area of research generally
- to make sure that I do not miss things
- to make my presentations more exciting

Review skill experience
- no ideas at all – help!

How can I develop it?
- brainstorm with friends each half term
- allow myself a good break each lunchtime
- read texts with an eye to how ideas are ordered

Where do I go next?
- *carry out a focus review next week*
- *pay Paul back for the brainstorming*

Presentation skills

Why do I need it?
- terrified of presentations
- not sure that I can get my points across well

Review skill experience
- did I present well at marketing meetings?
- what about my undergraduate seminars?

How can I develop it?
- get some practice – perhaps to friends?
- plan and prepare at least a week in advance

Where do I go next?
- *go to the study skills workshop*
- *volunteer for first term presentation*

Reading more productively

Why do I need it?
- find it difficult to decide what to read
- have too many books in my 'to read' pile

Continued

	• tend to overread in some areas
	• never seem to catch up
Review skill experience	• my reading skills as an undergraduate
	• reading at speed at work
	• I like reading!
How can I develop it?	• sort my reading material into cate-gories
	• return to library books that are of little use
	• make a reading chart to view progress
Where do I go next?	• *use two 'to read' notebooks, one for primary and one for secondary texts*
	• *make sure each week that every text to be read is in a notebook and mark them off as I get through them*

Our student may choose to produce one of these inventories each month, or she may use a separate sheet for each skill area and then add to it and revise it throughout her course. Whichever method she chooses, it is worth analysing what each of the completed boxes is intended to achieve. By identifying the reasons behind her need to develop a skill ('Why do I need it?'), she will be motivated to work on it: there is no point in just assuming that you need to develop every possible skill area without being clear about how it might help you in your course. These reasons will change over time and this box will help to keep you focused on the demands of your course.

By reviewing her existing strengths in each skill area ('Review skill experience'), she will ensure that she does not waste any of her past experience. This box will allow her to bring together her past life and her postgraduate life and although sometimes she will not be able to think of anything to put in this box (as in 'Thinking creatively' in this example), the space will allow her to add anything helpful as it occurs to her.

The suggestions in the 'How can I develop it?' section are calls to action. They are not vague ideas about what she would like to do in the future, but rather concrete plans that are achievable in a short space of time. By working to a relatively short timescale here she can gauge how well she is progressing. Once she has begun to work on her skill areas in the early stages of her course, she can include more ambitious, long-term plans in this section.

This development plan is all about ticking the boxes, really feeling that you are getting somewhere because you can see that you have carried out your plans and moved forwards. However, it will not work for you if it remains static: it should be part of a cumulative process. The final box for each skill ('Where do I go next?') is therefore vital. This allows our student to develop her next skills inventory, within which she will record the results of the actions that she had planned here and review what still needs to be done. As she becomes stronger in some areas, she might decide to include other skills on which she would like to work, always keeping in mind that this is a process of enrichment that will continue until the last day of her course and beyond.

Improving your skills base and creating an impressive skills portfolio by the conclusion of your course is largely under your control. It will reassure you that you are in charge of your development and it will support you in your research, but you do not have to work on it in isolation. Your supervisor is there to guide and encourage you, to be enthusiastic about your strengths and gentle with your weaknesses: this is going to be the most important academic relationship that you develop as a postgraduate.

Spot guide

Key points to remember from this chapter:

- analyse your existing skills base
- assess your needs in terms of skills development
- learn how to read productively
- improve the ways in which you articulate your ideas
- learn how to write persuasively
- problem-solving is vital to your success
- oral presentations must be mastered
- thinking creatively, laterally and as widely as possible is essential
- planning will form the basis of the management of your course
- produce a skills inventory in order to enhance your skills base

5 Working with your Supervisor

Troubleshooting guide

Read this chapter for help in the following areas:

- if you are in a position to choose a supervisor for your research
- if you want to know how your supervisor can be of most help to you
- if you have not had a supervisor for your work before
- if you are unsure about the type of support you can expect from your supervisor
- if you are unclear about how a supervision works
- if you want to exploit every opportunity open to you on your course
- if you are keen to develop a good working relationship with your supervisor
- if you find it difficult to take criticism
- if you want to change direction in your research and are worried about what to do next
- if you would like a glimpse of life from your supervisor's point of view

---

Working with a supervisor can feel rather strange in the beginning; this is probably the first time that you have worked so closely or over such a prolonged period with one academic. This chapter will help you to establish a productive working relationship with your supervisor and maintain it over time. It is not a working partnership that you can neglect, as you will need the help of your supervisor in so many ways, but neither is it an aspect of your postgraduate course that should cause you too much anxiety: your supervisor is a professional, keen to help and knowledgeable about the system within which you are both working.

► How to begin

The issue of choosing a supervisor was touched upon in Chapter 2, where the advantages of finding an expert in your field were discussed. If you are given a choice of supervisor, you will need to think carefully about your options and avoid rushing into a decision. You may have little idea at the outset of your course about how to choose a supervisor but there are several factors that you could consider.

Area of expertise
You may feel that this is obvious: of course your supervisor will be an expert in your field of interest, otherwise he or she would not be appointed as your supervisor. In reality the situation can be more complex than this; you might be studying a field that is so narrow or unusual that there is nobody available who perfectly matches your research needs, or perhaps a supervisor has expressed an interest in working within your area. Neither of these situations need be a problem, but they will have a bearing on how the relationship develops, so it is worth checking your library catalogue to find out what books your supervisor has published. Do not be put off if the catalogue only lists one publication: it could be that your supervisor tends to produce articles and academic papers or contributes to collections of essays rather than writing complete books and this information will usually be available to you via CD-ROM catalogues of publications. Having said that, if you have a supervisor who has published very little, it might be that he or she has only recently gained a doctorate and this has advantages and disadvantages which will be discussed next.

Experience
Although it is logical to assume that the more experience your supervisor has, both as an academic and a supervisor, the better this will be for you, take a moment to think it through before you jump in. An experienced supervisor will be familiar with the system and so will be in a good position to support you; an established academic with a reputation will also be able to help you with your academic networking and, perhaps, your future career. However, such a supervisor might be in great demand, with several postgraduates to supervise at any one time, which might leave you feeling as if you are permanently in a queuing system taking up time for which others are competing. The issue of how many postgraduates are under the care of your potential supervisor is an important one: you might benefit from the camaraderie of working as a group with your fellow supervisees, or you might feel that there is never enough time for you. A less experienced super-

visor may not be so familiar with the academic maze, but you might benefit from an energetic, fresh approach to the supervisory relationship and an enthusiastic commitment to getting it right.

Track record

Expertise in an academic field does not necessarily equate to experience as a supervisor. It is a good idea, if you can, to talk with someone who is currently working with the academic in question. There is nothing like inside knowledge to clear your mind and help you to make a decision, but be systematic about this. Just asking the general question 'is this supervisor any good?' is unlikely to help you much. As well as being unfair to the supervisor, the response you get is likely to be coloured by the immediate experience of your colleague: 'Yes, I have a great supervisor' (your colleague has just had a rare and productive supervision); 'I wouldn't choose this supervisor again' (your colleague is at a crucial stage of research and the supervisor has, unusually, taken a week to respond to an email). You would do better to have specific questions ready that relate to your particular needs: does the supervisor tend to be available in the vacations? How often might you expect a supervision? Is the supervisor keen on email communication? Does he or she have inspirational ideas or find creative solutions to problems? By being precise you will ensure that you get the information which you need before you make a commitment.

Availability

It would be unreasonable to expect your supervisor to be at your beck and call at all times, but availability will impact upon your relationship. You know how you work best. If you feel strongly that you will need supervisions (that is, one-to-one sessions with your supervisor) at least three or four times a term, you will be put off if you find that your proposed supervisor only sees postgraduates once a term, but there are ways around this problem, so try not to exclude a lecturer from your list of possible supervisors simply on this basis. It is more important to know whether the supervisor is going to be available for the whole of your course or whether sabbatical leave (that is, research leave that can last up to a year) is planned. It is also useful to know whether your scheduled time at university will coincide with that of your supervisor. It will be difficult for you both if your supervisor only comes into the department for two days a week and those are the days that you are unable to attend; make sure in advance that your available times for supervisions are compatible and that you can be fairly sure that your supervisor will also be available for minor queries on a regular basis.

Personality

This is a difficult one. Your supervisor may not become a friend; indeed, this might be a bad idea if you want to make the most of the relationship. However, if you find your supervisor a difficult person to get along with, this is likely to hinder your relationship. This is nobody's fault, but you do need to consider the basics before you go ahead with one specific supervisor. Think about your existing relationship, if your supervisor is already one of your lecturers or seminar tutors. Do you find it easy to talk through research problems? Are you made to feel confident enough to voice your ideas? Do you find the explanations that you are offered easy to understand? Do you feel that the lecturer has a realistic grasp of your abilities and the challenges that you face? If your answer to any of these questions is 'no', you need to consider whether this is the right supervisor for you. If you answer 'yes' to these questions, then try not to be put off just because you would find it difficult to chat over tea together. You can have a valuable relationship with a supervisor who you never meet except in the relatively formal setting of a lecture, seminar or supervision. You might not discuss your personal lives at all (unless these are relevant to your academic progress) and this is perfectly normal and no hindrance to a productive working relationship. In my time as an inexperienced researcher I remember one tutor who descended into Latin at moments of stress or confusion, another whose seminars were always fascinating but rarely to the point and yet another who was so erudite that I felt that I would never be able to say anything of value in the seminar, however well I had covered the subject in my preparation. I went on to enjoy the support that all these academics had to offer, but I was pleased not to have to face them as supervisors in the early stages of my research!

This list of considerations is similar to the checklist that an employer might use to vet potential employees and this is misleading, in that of course you are not in a position to choose a supervisor as if you were choosing your own personal employee who will be devoted to nothing other than your success as a postgraduate. It also overlooks the most important characteristic of any potential supervisor: enthusiasm. If an academic is happy to supervise you, keen and ready to support your efforts and prepared to spend a lot of time thinking about your research, finding information for you and pointing you in the right direction, then you are in the fortunate position of knowing that you will have a staunch ally in the management of your course. Whether or not you are able to choose your supervisor, it is important to take an active part in the relationship from the outset. You could use the points listed in this chapter to set your own agenda: what are your expectations? What do you need from your supervisor? What are you able to offer? How might you ensure that the relationship runs smoothly? If you can set your own agenda and meet your supervisor for the first time with a clear idea of what you will need and what you think you can reasonably expect, you will save yourself valuable time and effort in the future and minimise the possibility of confusion.

▶ What you can expect from your supervisor

Too many postgraduates spend precious time worrying about just how much support they can expect from their supervisors, both in terms of practical help and the wider academic and emotional support they might need. You do not have the time to worry about this: instead, you need to be clear about what is on offer and then work at making the most of it. In an attempt to demystify the supervision process, I have listed below the areas that tend to cause most confusion and given some guidelines as to what you might expect.

Supervisions

These are one-to-one sessions (very occasionally, they may include several students) in which your supervisor will talk through the specific challenges you are facing. This might include talking with you about the overall shape of your dissertation or thesis or the direction in which you are moving within one particular area of your research. They are your chance to get the highest possible level of support for your work, so be prepared to ask questions and seek clarification about anything that remains unclear to you. Supervisions might be a trial to you in the early days; you are unsure about what to expect and it can be an intense experience to sit for an hour or so with your supervisor talking through research which might be rather hazy to you as you develop your ideas. Your supervisor should put you at your ease and many of your early sessions will be quite general in nature, so they should not be viewed as a test of some sort: they are wholly for your benefit and should be seen as such.

The secret of successful supervisions is to prepare yourself for them in advance. In this way you are able to take some control of the supervision process and you will ensure that each supervision answers your specific questions. Try not to see supervisions in the same light as the termly meetings that undergraduates have with their tutors. A supervision is so much more than this: it is a time in which your supervisor should be fully focused on your needs, your ideas and the challenges that you face and in this way they will come to underpin everything that you do.

Written work

When you have to produce assessed work, your supervisor can help you to develop the shape of the piece and can guide you as to research that you could do and publications that might be of use to you. You will be expecting this support, but do not be surprised if you are also asked to produce more general written work in preparation for your supervisions. Supervisors are aware that they have relatively little face-to-face time with you compared to the work you are putting into your course and they will want to make the most of the time you do have together. For this reason, you might be asked to produce a written record of your research, to be given to your supervisor before each supervision. This might take the form of a brief progress report on, for example, the publications you have been exploring or the primary material you have found. You might be asked to revise your overall plan in writing so it can be discussed or produce a draft chapter of your dissertation or thesis so it can be assessed by both of you.

If you are busy researching, this can seem like a waste of time but it will always be to your benefit. The art of producing an extended piece of research is to keep your ideas flowing. You might feel that you are spending fruitless hours writing up synopses of each text you are exploring, but in fact what you will be doing is developing your academic talents. You will record your ideas and note connections and research paths in your notes, of course, but by writing them out in this extended way you are forcing yourself to practise articulating these ideas in writing and you will always have a record of how your ideas are developing. Trying out ideas in writing is always more satisfactory than just jotting them down in the margins of your notes. For most postgraduates, it is only in this way that they can fully grasp the direction in which their research is leading them. There is a further benefit to this process: when you come to write up your dissertation or thesis, you will be so grateful that you have a record of work that you now have to revisit, but that you have not thought about in detail for a year or more. You will also find that, occasionally, you can incorporate whole sections of these synopses into your final work, which is a great relief when you are faced with having to produce thousands of words in what seems like an alarmingly short space of time.

Networking

Academic life relies to some extent upon networking. If you are not intending to pursue an academic career beyond your current postgraduate course, at first sight this may appear to be of little interest to you, but academic networking is useful in many ways. You might, for example, find another postgraduate who is working in a field tangential to your own, who could share research sources with you but only if your supervisor has kept you up to date with the academic conferences taking place in your area of interest. The breadth of support that you can access might depend upon networking. If, for example, you are examining the impact of apartheid on the legal system of South Africa in the 1980s, you might be supervised within the history department of your university or college. However, you will benefit from the support of the law and international relations departments and you might also like to attend a few lectures on courses such as 'South Africa and the US: a comparative approach to race law'; 'The development of the American novel' and 'Iconography in the media age'. There will always be something that you miss, but if you let your supervisor know that you have a wide-ranging interest in all aspects of your field and are keen to attend every event that might relate to it, you will be able to find out about most of the available opportunities.

Sometimes your networking will be less specific. Perhaps you would like to meet regularly with other postgraduates or take advantage of an exchange scheme with other universities; these are just two examples of the ways in which your supervisor can enrich your academic life. Again, it is simply a case of making it known during supervisions that you are interested in every possible opportunity.

Opportunities

Postgraduates are usually unaware of the importance of getting published early: it can be months, even years, before an article appears in print. This will be discussed in more detail in Chapter 9, but at this stage you need to be proactive: do not assume that your work is not good enough to be published. Early chapters of your thesis or dissertation may, with a little working up, become excellent articles, so do not shy away from discussing this possibility with your supervisor. You will also notice posters (or receive emails) that include a 'call for papers', a request that anyone who is interested in producing a paper to give at a conference contact the organisers. You are usually given notice of conferences many weeks before the event, so you have plenty of time to discuss with your supervisor whether you should offer a paper, the research that will be of most interest to the conference delegates and the ways in which you might write such a paper.

Your supervisor may be able to arrange for you to undertake some undergraduate teaching during your course. This might be a way of earning a little extra money whilst you carry out your research, so do not be afraid to ask about the possibility. Whether you are paid or not, talking through your research with undergraduates or giving a paper to a group of your fellow postgraduates is a great way to test out your ideas on an audience and develop your academic skills.

Research skills

Nobody is going to assume that you are an expert on producing a dissertation or a thesis: you have yet to do this. Equally, you will not be expected to come up with the last word in your area: good research tends to raise as many questions as it answers. However, you have been accepted onto your course and you will have the basic skills you need: you can write essays or reports and, perhaps, extended pieces of work, you can articulate your ideas and produce a logical argument based upon evidence. What you may feel less confident about is the process of undertaking research and presenting it coherently. Where do you go for material? How can you remain focused? What should you discard? How can you tell if a theory has been discredited? How will you be able to produce a reasonable dissertation or thesis plan? In addition to these general questions, you might have your own specific areas of concern: how can you improve your writing skills? How do you prepare to give a presentation? How can you make the most of the Internet and CD-ROM resources? Make a note of these issues as they arise and take them to your supervisor at your next meeting. Embarrassment is the greatest single hindrance to a productive relationship. You might feel shy about revealing that you have a problem with grammar or spelling, but it is no trouble to your supervisor to point you in the direction of study skills workshops that will solve your problem. You are not going to be familiar with the work of every leading expert in your field, indeed you may not have heard of several of them, but your supervisor will expect this and be happy to expand your reading plan with you. You might assume that you should know exactly where to go next in your research, but why should you? You are not the expert, but your supervisor is, and it is this expertise that you must rely upon.

Ethics

It is not always easy to grasp the range of ethical considerations you will need to take into account as your work progresses, but your supervisor will be acutely aware of this issue and will be able to offer you valuable advice. Although in some areas a clearly defined code of ethics will apply (for example if you are using human tissue within scientific experimentation or using data drawn from individuals within social science research), in other areas of activity there might be less clarity. The best way to approach this is to assume that, even if you are aware of an ethical code of practice in your area, it is still advisable to discuss this issue with your supervisor as your work develops, particularly as you might have to have ethical approval from your university to carry out certain elements of your research. If you are in any way uncertain about the ethical implications of the work you are carrying out, do not rely solely upon written guidelines but use them in conjunction with the advice and experience that your supervisor can offer you.

Ideas

Your supervisor may or may not be good at coming up with ideas. Some supervisors seem to have endless reserves of inspiration, whilst others will simply reflect upon the ideas you generate. On the downside, inspirational supervisors might lack the attention to detail and considered reflection of your work that you need. A positive benefit of a reflective supervisor might be that you are given plenty of support in how to turn your ideas into workable hypotheses and effective chapters of your thesis or dissertation. If you know that you are the sort of person who finds it difficult to get out of a mindset that is going nowhere and you will need to be fed lots of ideas as you go along, but your supervisor is not an 'ideas person', take control of the situation. If you can produce a few ideas yourself, however sketchy or tangential to your research, this will encourage your supervisor to join with you in thinking up more. Even if your supervisor is not naturally very creative, you will find that experience tells and ideas or theories that are familiar to your supervisor will be new and exciting to you.

Your search for new ideas and creative solutions to research problems need not be restricted to your supervisions. Your supervisor may know of discussion groups and general postgraduate research seminars that could help you. If these are scarce at your university or college, it might be possible for your supervisor to put you in touch with study groups in other institutions or direct you towards academic websites with notice boards and chat rooms that could be useful to you. Throughout your postgraduate life, your supervisor need not be your only source of support but is likely to be your first port of call.

Emotional support

This is always a tricky subject. In an ideal world you would breeze through your postgraduate course, with never a doubt about your direction and a lasting certainty about both your abilities and the shape your final dissertation or thesis will take. At those times when you might feel overwhelmed by your workload, your supervisor will be instantly available and ready with tea and sympathy. In practice, your postgraduate experience is likely to be a mixture of these two extremes. There will be times when you feel on top of the course (and so on top of the world) and everything is falling into place with very little effort. At other points on your journey, you will inevitably feel less sure of yourself and your research, unclear of your overall aims and uncertain as to where to go next. At both of these points your supervisor will be an asset to you. When things are going well, you will have the time and energy to discuss your future, new avenues of research or how to prepare a bibliography. When things are going badly, your supervisor will offer you practical and academic guidance and also, hopefully, a level of emotional support.

The key to managing this potentially awkward aspect of the relationship is to speak up when you feel vulnerable. The more organised you are, the more you appear to be in control of your research, the less inclined your supervisor will be to offer what might seem to be unnecessary emotional encouragement. In fact, we all need praise and reassurance, however organised we are, so make this clear to your supervisor, who may feel diffident about this area. If you ask for encouragement ('Do you really think this chapter works?' 'I found this so much harder to do than I had expected.' 'Although I look organised, I have slaved for hours over just this one essay.'), then your supervisor will know that you welcome emotional support. As noted earlier, a supervision is not a test, and you will want to leave your supervisions feeling better than when you entered them. Your supervisor is not a mind reader and may genuinely think you are having no problems, may feel that you would shun too much encouragement or that you are unapproachable because you appear to be so organised. If none of these statements is true of you, make sure that your supervisor knows or you might be left feeling needlessly isolated.

▶ Developing your relationship

Once you have established a working relationship with your supervisor, you will need to work within it as your research progresses. It might last for several years and you could return to your supervisor for advice and references for many years after the completion of your course, so it is worth taking the time and trouble to ensure that the relationship is not only maintained, but also developed and fostered. There are as many different supervisors as there are postgraduates to be supervised, but fundamental aspects of the relationship will be common to all.

Communication
You will have supervisions, but you will also have minor queries you want to raise with your supervisor during your research (Does he or she have a copy of a book you need? How should you divide the books in your bibliography list? Can you change the time of your next supervision?). If you regularly see your supervisor in the corridors of your department, it is tempting just to ask these question when you meet, but this can lead to your supervisor ducking into the photocopying room whenever you appear or you misunderstanding an answer in your haste. The best way to approach these

minor queries is to raise them by email. This has the advantage of ensuring that they are answered and it also leaves your supervisor free to think about what it is that you really need before answering. In this way you will receive an answer to your initial questions and also useful suggestions that will support the wider area of work that raised the question.

Having urged you to email your supervisor, there is one word of warning. Make sure that he or she is happy to work in this way. There will always be lecturers (as there are postgraduates) who are uncomfortable with this form of communication, rarely open their email box and will therefore take an impractical length of time to answer your questions. Some people do prefer to chat face to face or over the phone, so ask at your first meeting about how your supervisor prefers to work.

Getting beyond the criticism

Picture the scene: you are producing a dissertation on the phenomenon of crop circles in the 1990s. You have decided to look at patterns of incidence and the theories that might explain them. You also want to explore the ways in which they might impact economically and culturally upon local communities. During your last supervision you chatted about the possibility of including a section dealing with the theory held by some farmers and other interest groups that crop circles are produced by extraterrestrial interference. Enthused by the disucsssion, you then spend a week reading the literature that attaches to this theory and trying to place this in the context of your other data and hypotheses. You meet for your next supervision, keen by now to develop this into a whole chapter in your dissertation and your supervisor casually mentions having had second thoughts; the body of literature on this subject is so vast that it will distort the overall shape of the dissertation. This is followed by a suggestion that you include a mention of it only in footnotes. You smile, trying to be polite (this is, after all, an expert who is helping you), whereas you actually want to run screaming from the room. You are, naturally, disheartened that so much work can be discarded in one sentence, and you might feel foolish, given that you are still so keen on the idea.

Despite your understandable disappointment and frustration, you have to get past what appears to be criticism of your work and ideas. In fact, it might be perfectly sensible to reduce this aspect of your research to footnotes, but it can be difficult to see this at the time. If you are too upset, you will not be able to make the most of the supervision, so there are two things you must do to counterbalance this potential hurdle in your relationship. Firstly, expect to have to discuss and defend each idea at a supervision. Remember that your supervisor has not spent weeks working on an idea and is there to retain the overall shape clearly in mind and so help you to see the bigger picture. This does not mean that your supervisor is invariably right, but a large part of this relationship should be the testing of ideas and the questioning of work you have done: that is what your supervisor is for, and this process is essential to the production of the best work you can produce. Secondly, do not simply discard material that has been open to question. If you accept the point your supervisor has made, put your research on that aspect of your subject to one side, get on with other areas of research and then go back to reassess it in a few weeks' time, bearing in mind the comments your supervisor has made. One of the features of postgraduate research students find most difficult is the fact that their sphere of reference can change over time. Unlike other pieces of work you will have produced in your undergraduate or professional life, a dissertation or thesis is expected to evolve; your first plan may bear little relation to your final plan, which can be unnerving but necessary. You will become emotionally attached to some theories and ideas and this is not a bad thing, but if your supervisor is less enthusiastic, try to take the criticism (it is not a personal criticism of you), reassess your position and move on to other, more productive research.

Using your judgement
Having urged you to accept criticism and move beyond it, this is not to suggest that your supervisor will always be right. This is your research, your dissertation or thesis and there will be times when, by the very nature of things, you will be right. Your supervisor cannot see every aspect of your argument or necessarily see how it will fit into your scheme of things, particularly because you are unlikely to have produced a whole new plan whilst you are still working on undeveloped ideas. If you feel that an area of your research is being given too little chance to grow and develop or you are not putting your ideas across as well as you had hoped, explain to your supervisor that you need time to think about it before you abandon what could be vital work. You can then spend a little more time on it, although you will not want to spend too much time on an idea that has now been questioned, and then rework your plan, showing how this research is relevant to your new scheme and email a copy of the new plan to your supervisor. You might still find that you do not agree on its importance, but at least you will have had the chance to explain and it is most unlikely your supervisor would simply veto your idea at this stage. It is more probable that you will move ahead with the research, perhaps adapting your approach in the light of your supervisor's comments.

Your academic judgement is what will shape the overall structure of your dissertation or thesis. You may rightly assume that your supervisor, as the author perhaps of several books and articles, will have a more highly developed academic judgement than you, but it is impossible for a supervisor, however hard he or she tries, to get into your head to see exactly how you envisage your final work. You are carrying out the research, so you are in the best position to judge how important an area is going to become to your hypothesis; you have to produce the work, so you must be happy with your final plan. Your supervisor has a different style and knowledge base, and no two people would ever produce exactly the same plan for a similar piece of work. It would not be unusual if you were to create half a dozen plans before finding a final version that suits you and your supervisor will not be fazed by this. However, when you have reached the point where you feel happy with your plan, try to stick to it, incorporating your supervisor's ideas into it rather than changing the whole structure after each supervision. The key here is to be able to explain what you mean and what you intend to do, rather than always presuming that you must change your plan after every suggestion by your supervisor: this is your work, so make it your own by creating it from a plan that makes sense to you.

The need to exercise your own judgement extends to new areas of research. You will learn to take constructive criticism and your supervisor will be trying to generate ideas, inspire you and widen your horizons. However, it can be awkward if a suggestion made by your supervisor does not work out and you might hesitate to report back that you do not intend to develop the idea further, but this will not be met by disapproval. Your supervisor does not intend to be the expert in every aspect of your work; the suggestion was just that, a suggestion, and there will be no hard feelings if you decide to abandon it because it does not support your current research.

Changing direction

The plan for your dissertation or thesis will alter over time, with perhaps a growing emphasis on one area or the addition of a chapter as new material comes to light. This is a normal part of the creative process and should cause you no great concern. However, there might come a time when you begin to feel that a new direction is needed, your base hypothesis is flawed or inadequate and you will not being doing justice to your work until you make a radical change in direction, perhaps by altering the thrust of your plan entirely. This will not be an overnight decision. Instead, you will probably spend a week or so with a general feeling of unease as you find that each area on which you are working seems to support your new ideas more than your existing plan. Try not to allow this stage to extend beyond a couple of weeks. When, eventually, you decide to take the plunge and make a new plan, avoid the temptation to develop it fully and work all your material into it before sharing it with your supervisor. It is far better to arrange a meeting to discuss this new direction when you have no more than a draft revised plan in place. In this way your supervisor can guide you through the changes you want to make and discuss with you how your material will fit into the plan.

There are two practical reasons for revealing to your supervisor a change of direction relatively early in the process. You might be surprised at just how much time your supervisor spends thinking about your work: each article he or she reads or seminar or conference he or she attends will be grist to the mill and will be throwing up suggestions ready for your next supervision. It is therefore frustrating for your supervisor to find that you changed your mind about the overall direction of your research a fortnight before a supervision and did not mention it. Secondly, a change of direction might require a level of extended supervision, either by arranging for more frequent meetings whilst you work through the plan together, or by bringing in an additional supervisor from another department, and these things take time to arrange, time which you will not want to waste.

▶ Life from your supervisor's point of view

As a new postgraduate, independent research might be a new concept for you, indeed, academic life as a whole might be a novel experience and you will be concerned to make the most of it. You will have challenges, naturally, and you will also have the pleasure of finding out how good you are at working under your own steam, creating working hypotheses and finding new research questions. The subject will interest you and your supervisor is, of course, only too happy to help. Amongst all this excitement and sheer hard work it is worth thinking for a few moments about the process from your supervisor's point of view: this is a two-way relationship. Whilst you can reasonably expect an adequate level of support for your endeavours, if you foster the relationship you can get so much more out of it. All supervisors will differ in their attitude towards supervision, but these are some general considerations to take into account.

Being flexible
Remember that your supervisor is not being paid vast sums of money to supervise your work. He or she is doing it because it is an accepted part of the work of an academic, your research is of interest in itself and, hopefully, your supervisor enjoys talking through ideas with you. With this in mind, it is a good idea for you to adopt a flexible attitude towards the supervision that you receive. You should not feel awkward every time you need to see

your supervisor or feel that you are taking up too much valuable time, but if your supervisor needs to alter the timing of a supervision or does not get around to answering your emails within 24 hours, you can safely assume that there is a good reason for this.

Everybody is entitled to the occasional bad day. If you find a supervision uninspiring, it is not necessarily anybody's fault, it could just be that your supervisor is distracted by other work, so try not to read too much into it. It does not mean that he or she is bored by what you are doing or harbouring doubts about either your progress or the general direction of your research, so try not to worry too much and send an email a few days later confirming what was said and what direction you are now taking: you are likely to get a far more enthusiastic response than you had expected.

Giving feedback

One of the pleasures for a supervisor is the way in which, late on a Friday afternoon, you receive an email with an attachment that outlines your supervisee's work for the week, with details of the texts that have been explored, the primary material that has been sifted and a series of suggestions as to how this research might fit into the overall plan of the dissertation or thesis. Whilst daily reports on your progress would be excessive and might leave your supervisor feeling obliged to give your work more time than is possible, regular feedback is always a good thing. It will serve two purposes: it will keep your existence in the forefront of your supervisor's mind and allow your supervisor to keep up with your thought processes and research ideas, so that you are on the same wavelength each time you have a supervision. In your first meeting, find out how often your supervisor would like to hear from you with feedback on your progress and do not forget to include other news, such as whether you are going to attend a conference or are intending to give a paper at an event at which you will both be present. Most importantly, let your supervisor know if you are enjoying yourself. Supervisors expect to see their postgraduates when things go wrong, but it is uplifting to receive the occasional email or note confirming that things are going well and you are happy in what you are doing.

The paperwork

It would be an unusual supervisor who revelled in producing the piles of paperwork that will become attached to your postgraduate course. Administrative forms have to be completed, research reports must be compiled and progress has to be monitored in writing. This is unlikely to be a favourite job with either of you, although you might benefit from recording your work in this way, so make sure that every form you have to complete is returned to your supervisor in double quick time.

If you are uncertain about how to fill out a form, or the purpose that it is intended to serve, check first with your departmental secretary, who will probably know about all the forms associated with your course. This will save you wasting valuable supervision time talking through forms that may not be adding materially to your postgraduate experience. Keep a copy of all forms so that you are not caught out if they get lost: it is frustrating to spend a morning filling out a form only to find that you have to repeat the process a week later. It is also a good idea to check that forms which have to be submitted within a certain time have actually reached their destination: your supervisor may not be as good at administration as at supervising. Once the paperwork is out of the way, you can both get back to the far more enjoyable task of carrying out the research.

And if things go wrong . . .

We all have times when nothing seems to go right. You are trying to complete a chapter of your dissertation or thesis and at the same time you are preparing a paper for a conference. You can guarantee that this is the week when the car will break down, your boss (if you are working) will pile on the work and the phone will ring just as you leave the house. This need not be a problem; your supervisor is human too, and will not hold it against you if you cannot make a supervision or are unable to produce a report on your research in the timeframe that you discussed. The problem is not one of life getting in the way, but one of you then not letting your supervisor know that the world appears to be crumbling around you. If you cannot make a supervision, your supervisor will have plenty to get on with and is not going to worry about it, as long as you have made contact and arranged another appointment. Similarly, failing to hand in an ongoing research report is not going to impede your overall progress, but it will be a nuisance if your supervisor had set aside time at the weekend to look it over and it just fails to appear. If you cannot get a conference paper to go right, your supervisor can help you to rectify the problem with relative ease, but if you avoid discussing the issue until you are in a desperate state about it, the task is going to be far greater. Your supervisor is there to help: all you have to do is make the most of the support that is on offer.

Spot guide

Key points to remember from this chapter:

- if you can choose your supervisor, check:
  - area of expertise
  - experience as a supervisor
  - track record
  - availability
  - and, most importantly, enthusiasm
- supervisions are not a test, they are a chance to discuss your ideas and raise your questions
- try to broaden your range of research and learning opportunities with the help of your supervisor
- begin to network as soon as possible: you need a support structure
- you are not expected to be an expert in every aspect of your course
- try not to take criticism in supervisions personally: your supervisor is there to help you
- let your supervisor know if you are struggling in any part of your course
- find out how best to communicate with your supervisor
- develop your academic judgement with the support of your supervisor
- if you change direction significantly in your research, tell your supervisor fairly promptly
- try to be flexible about the practicalities of your supervision
- get the administration out of the way quickly: keep copies of all paperwork
- occasionally let your supervisor know that you are enjoying your research!

6 Managing your Course

Troubleshooting guide

Read this chapter for help in the following areas:

- if you want to become an active note-taker
- if you are concerned about how to keep useful and relevant records
- if you are not sure how to take control of your reading and research
- if you have difficulty in making connections between disparate strands of your research
- if you are not clear about how to make the most of all the opportunities open to you
- if you are anxious that you might be missing leads in your research tasks
- if you have trouble keeping your research paths in order
- if you are concerned about forgetting references or ideas
- if you would like help in tackling time management
- if you find it difficult to juggle the competing demands in your life
- if you keep running out of time to do all that you would like to do

Undertaking a postgraduate course is a varied experience: you will be attending seminars, lectures and supervisions; you will be asked to take on board the views and theories of a range of lecturers and, perhaps, guest speakers; and you will also be forming your own opinions and carrying our independent research. This can be confusing, not because you will have difficulty in understanding each aspect of your course, but because you have to find an effective way of pulling together these strands into a cohesive whole that will support your overall aims.

▶ Taking control

The way to achieve this cohesion is to take control as early as you can by developing your own systems of note-taking, record-keeping and research-tagging. You will create your own systems but there are several techniques you can employ which will help to keep you on track and can be expanded as your course progresses.

Note-taking

The production of useful notes is an art in itself, one you might have developed in earlier study situations. As a postgraduate, you need to see your note-taking as an active process, one that continues beyond the initial learning situation. You will have notes from lectures and seminars, but you will also be making notes from your own sources. Try to keep them as uniform as possible, using a standard format to indicate books you must read, ideas you want to explore further and theories you want to consider. You will have a growing set of notes, which will be revisited periodically: it is a good idea to work through your notes each week to reassess what they are offering you. This has two clear advantages for you. There will not be time when you are writing up a piece of work to wade through reams of undigested notes in the hope that you will be able to pick out rapidly those points that are of most use to you. By reworking your notes you will have to read through only a fraction of your initial work in order to locate those facts and ideas that are relevant to the work you have in hand. The second advantage is that reworking your notes will help you to focus. It will throw up new ideas, reaffirm theories you already hold and help you to avoid missing research opportunities.

Let us take as an example a set of notes made during a lecture on the subject of publication in the seventeenth century. The lecture itself was rather general in nature, and might have been a waste of time as our postgraduate is intending to focus in her assessed essay on female authored publications and is not sure whether there will be much useful material in the lecture. However, she is an active note-taker and has produced a relatively comprehensive set of notes, reworked after the event, part of which is reproduced here.

6 Dec 2003	Title: Publication in the seventeenth century
Dr Becker email address?	C17 publications were usually of a religious nature. Many printers were involved: there was a need to make money, although some publications were printed at the expense of the author or his/her representatives. *Why? Commemoration? Family pride? Religious propaganda?*
	Popular ballads were produced in broadsheet format and sold cheaply to the masses. *How were women involved in this?*
	The advent of the printing press had made widespread publication possible.
Intro	The tradition of manuscript circulation continued despite the development of print. *Am I going to include manuscripts? If not, mention it somewhere?*
Research task	It can be difficult to work out which authors wrote which books as they are often only identified by initials. *Could be useful – go back and check on this . . .*
	Books were sometimes seen as monuments to the author, such as when a clergyman died and his sermons were published.
Read this!	My book on the subject mentions some issues of publication at this time. *What book?*

Continued

> Chapbooks were often said to be 'moral instruction manuals for the masses'.
> *Is this her quote? What are 'chapbooks'?*
>
> The Church was keen to take advantage of the possibilities of publication.
> My idea   *In a culture that mistrusted female speech, could women appear in print if they were supporting religious propaganda – was this a chance for them to be heard?*

As you can see, the initial lecture notes are only of marginal value to our student. She has left plenty of space between the points that were made (shown here in Roman) so that she can revisit the notes and add her own comments (given here in italics). She has used the margin to organise the set of tasks that arise from this lecture. By noting the date of the lecture and the lecturer's name, she can be sure that she will remember the event and can get hold of the lecturer in the future if she needs to check anything, such as, in this case, the source of the quote that was given. Some notes she can easily identify as being of use to her only as passing comments in her essay, such as the 'intro' note, reminding her to mention whether or not she is using manuscript sources. Her research task will be entered into her research notebook (which will be discussed in detail later in this chapter) and her reading list will now include the book that was mentioned.

Perhaps the most important marginal note that she has made is the comment 'my idea'. It is so frustrating to see a clever idea in your notes and have no recollection, months after the event, whether it was yours or not. As already mentioned, plagiarism is the gravest offence in academia and always brings with it the severest penalties, which can leave you in the position of either having to go back and trace an idea (almost impossible, in most cases) or leaving it out of your work altogether, just in case you are plagiarising by mistake. By securing your own ideas in marginal notes in this way, you can use them with confidence and build upon them as your research progresses.

In addition to the marginal notes, our student has almost doubled the original lecture notes with her own thoughts and instructions to herself. These instructions take the form of questions, reminding her to check on terms with which she is unfamiliar, suggesting new areas of source material that she can explore and leading her to develop her existing ideas. Her initial notes would have been useful to her: these expanded notes will become the starting point for action.

Record-keeping

You will be used to keeping basic records: reading lists you have customised, lecture notes you have filed and copies of your essays and coursework. The usefulness of these records can be dramatically increased if you keep by you, throughout your course, two record-keeping notebooks. Ideally these will be hardback, A5 notebooks in which you will make a note of all the books you intend to read. One will be for primary sources (that is, research material that you will study in the original, condensed results of your experiments and so on), the other will be kept for secondary sources (that is, books and articles of which you have heard and in which you have an interest, believing that they might back up your primary research). You will note each publication or piece of source material that you come across in these books, and your reading lists will be transferred into them so that you have one, central record of the reading you hope to do in the course of your research. If you include the full reference to each book or article (that is, title, author, title and details of full publication if it is an article, date and place of publication and publisher), these record books will be a blessing when you come to produce a bibliography.

These notebooks are going to become the heart of your research activities, for three reasons. Firstly, they will be your guarantee that you are in control of your work, aware of what you have to achieve as you move forwards. Secondly, they bring together all the sources you are offered and so eradicate confusion: they are your unique reference index. Thirdly, they allow you to spend time doing something other than direct research. Having noted the details of each publication, leave a couple of lines blank. When you are too tired to look at yet another book or are waiting for a publication to become available, you can spend a satisfying couple of hours noting the library references beneath each title, with a note as to when you ordered the book, if it is not in your library. When you have read the book or examined the source material, or perhaps glanced at it and discarded it (this will happen relatively often), you can then cross through the reference in your notebook to show that you have covered it. You will still be able to see the details for inclusion in your bibliographies, but you will be in a position to check back and feel the satisfaction of having completed a whole page of references. Once you have done this, you can snip off the corner of that page, to indicate that it has been covered. This process is deliberately empowering: it will reduce your anxiety, remind you of how much work you have done and show you at a glance how much is left to do.

Research-tagging

The process by which you will keep control of your research paths is similar to that outlined above for your reading. Again, you will have an A5 hardback notebook, in which you will note every research idea you have and also incidental comments you have noted from your lectures, seminars and supervisions. These might include the names of historical figures whose work you want to look up or research ideas you might be able to develop. You will also include 'alert notes', such as a warning that a piece of work has been discredited or reminders (as in the manuscript comment in the lecture notes above) that you need to address an issue in your work. This book will be messy and this is all to the good. It is where you will begin the journey of working through your ideas, developing your own train of thought and exploring new areas of source material. There will be some overlap between the books, in that the publications of authors you mention in passing in this book will be transferred to your reading notebooks once you have discovered the titles. You will also use this book to help you to make connections and these will be central to your success in managing your course.

▶ Making connections

Being able to make meaningful and relevant connections between disparate pieces of research is one of the most challenging aspects of a postgraduate course. It is possible to complete an undergraduate course having made relatively few connections beyond the obvious ones that have been pointed out to you. As a postgraduate, you will have to make connections between what might often seem at first sight to be very unconnected pieces of research. If, for example, you are producing a dissertation looking at the effects of civil wars in Africa, you will expect to examine the ways in which different regimes were supported, tacitly or otherwise, by the Soviet Union or the USA during the Cold War. When your supervisor suggests that you attend a lecture on postcolonial literature, you might not initially see it as valuable to the work you are doing. If you take just basic notes you might not get much beyond this initial view, but if you can keep an open mind and create active lecture notes as was suggested above, you will realise that you must go much further back in history and assess the impact of decolonisation in Africa. It is at this point that you will discover that the former colonial powers set the boundaries of African states according to their areas of interest rather than tribal areas, and thus planted the seeds for civil strife. Once you have done this, you will be able to turn to your reading notebooks, in which you have listed some of the writers mentioned in the lecture. You are not producing a literature essay, so you will not rely heavily upon these writers, but you might choose to quote them at the opening of each chapter of your dissertation, just to set the scene.

The problem with trying to make connections as your work progresses is that, inevitably, if you fail to make a connection, you have no idea that you have failed: after all, you have not made the connection because you did not notice it in the first place. There has to be a limit to the number of connections you can make during your course and there is no way to guarantee that you do not miss anything, but there are methods you can employ to ensure that you notice, and then use, most of the relevant connections available to you. These methods are discussed in turn below.

Keep your research notebooks updated

This is good advice for all sorts of reasons, not least of which is to reduce your workload when it comes to writing a major piece of coursework. The secret is not just to keep them updated, but also to include every thought and idea you have, from your initial research ideas to your fully developed ideas. It really does not matter that many of your ideas will be crossed out by the end of your course: the very act of writing them down will keep them in your mind so that you remain alert for connections that might consolidate or extend them into useful areas of research.

Attend any event that might help you

You are unlikely to have time to attend every seminar or lecture in your university that might be of passing interest or go to each conference that looks enticing. If you were to do this, your personalised timetable would soon become so full as to be of little real help to you. However, many postgraduates work only within their own departments, so simply by looking around and assessing what is on offer throughout your university or college you will be in a far better position than most to make connections. This is particularly important if you are undertaking a distance or open learning course: becoming involved in every possible learning opportunity will stop you feeling isolated, as well as helping you to make research connections.

Join discussion groups

The value of discussion groups has already been discussed, but you can do more than simply attend them. Even if you are not involved in running such a group, it is a good idea to suggest that those attending the group give short presentations, perhaps five minutes or so, on the progress of their research. This might be a requirement on your course in any case, and these presentations will be useful to you. Although many of the presentations will be of no more than general interest, it will only take one or two passing comments to show you how the research of your fellow students could help to shape your own thoughts.

Develop studying partnerships

Connections can sometimes be difficult to spot once you are embroiled in your subject, perhaps focused on producing a piece of coursework or preparing for a seminar presentation. If you can find a studying partner, this will be one of the most valuable relationships within your postgraduate course. By arranging to meet occasionally, maybe each week, you can talk through the work that you are doing. You need not both be studying on the same course: in fact, it can be more inspirational to get an outsider's opinion. It is a useful discipline to have to prepare something for these sessions and in this way they can become very much like secondary supervisions. The questions your studying partner asks about your work ('Why is that so?', 'How do you know that this theory will work?', 'Is that the same point that you were making in your last coursework?') will lead you to make connections that you might not have seen by yourself.

Always check contents pages and bibliographies

You will spend much of your time as a postgraduate reading just part of each book that you discover or scouring a journal for a single article. This is as it should be, but try not to ignore the valuable connections that have already been made for you. By checking the contents page of a book or journal, you can see what other avenues have been explored in your subject area: if an author or journal editor has found connections, you might just as well use them. If you check the bibliography of a book, you might be surprised at how widely the author has read around the subject. Many of the texts included in a bibliography will be irrelevant to your needs, but if you spot a text that has no obvious connection with the book's contents, check it out. It is in these unlikely places that you can find really useful connections.

Internet and catalogue connections

Although I have urged you to avoid spending too long browsing the Internet in a haphazard way, it is worth occasionally spending thirty minutes or so browsing, with a view to making connections. Type in your search term, either on the Internet or library cataloguing system, and see what comes up. Remember that you are not intending to read each site or look up each book, you are simply trying to see what connections other academics have made within your subject area. By the end of the session, you will have jotted down a series of random notes and these will give you potential connections to bear in mind as you develop your ideas. Once you have worked through your ideas in more depth, you can return to the Internet or catalogue to look in far more detail at the material on offer. This exercise also brings variety to your tasks, an advantage as you work through your research.

Disciplines can mix

I would not suggest that including a poem in a science dissertation or incorporating a mathematical theorem into a literary analysis is the way to guarantee success, but making connections is all about keeping an open mind. We all become so used to working within a heavily defined sphere of reference that we can easily overlook the ways in which the work of other disciplines can enhance our own output. This is not an obvious path to tread, but if you try to keep an open mind about the options available to you, it is possible to make the most unlikely connections. For example, science may be a branch of endeavour that is separated today from the arts and humanities, but a few hundred years ago the two disciplines were far more interconnected, so studying the history of either will require you to make interdisciplinary connections that are unusual today. A more subtle problem can be the way in which postgraduates can shy away from other disciplines. You have a supervisor in your subject area and it is in this area that your work will principally lie, but if you are offered the chance to work within another discipline for a short time, do not be put off: it could provide you with novel and exciting connections.

▶ Keeping on track

In developing your research management techniques, you might consider producing a 'research sheet' for each area you are exploring. Your reading and research notebooks will be covering many different research areas; as you are working on one area, perhaps for an assessed essay, you will simultaneously be thinking about your main dissertation or thesis, noting down references for both. One of the greatest dangers in postgraduate research is that of simply losing your way, forgetting texts that you meant to look up and overlooking areas of research that you intended to explore. The solution to this problem might seem obvious: you will simply make a plan of your coursework, essay or dissertation as soon as you have a title in place. However, you need to develop the thinking skills mentioned in Chapter 4, forcing yourself to think laterally and creatively, and being flexible enough in your approach to allow a piece of work to develop under its own steam. If you rigidly control the plan for the work in its early stages, you run the risk of being unable to adapt and foster your research ideas.

Avoiding these problems is relatively simple, and becomes easier with practice. By entering the references and ideas for one piece of work onto a research sheet you can isolate them, thus ensuring that you do not miss anything. You will begin to see the emerging shape of your plan, but you will be able to alter that plan in your mind as your research progresses. This allows you to work in two stages: a research sheet which develops as you carry out your research, followed in the later stages by a draft plan you can discuss with your supervisor before producing a full plan.

I will return to the example of the postgraduate looking at female authored publications in the seventeenth century. She has agreed with her supervisor that the title of her assessed essay is to be 'Women in waiting: Seventeenth-century female authored publications.' She thinks that it is a catchy title, but knows that it will need some interpretation, so she begins her research sheet with an overview of what she is trying to say (this might change over time) and then pulls together research strands from her research notebook and notes down references from her reading notebooks.

Women in waiting: Seventeenth-century female authored publications

Intro
- not covering manuscript sources in much detail – just print publications
- history of print – problems of publication as somehow inappropriate for the nobility
- overview – publishing was a male-dominated activity in a patriarchal society and women had to wait in the wings, sneaking into publication where they could and using a male discourse to express themselves

opening sentence? make it sound better – less definite and more of a hypothesis

Part one?
- talk about research challenges, including women publishing under initials
- talk about history of women and writing, in brief

go back to the invention of the printing press
look at Shenner's work on women and writing
give example of T.C. and her 1640 poetry collection

- maybe link problems of female authored publications then and similar problems now? Are there any? Check back to undergraduate 'women and writing' course notes

Conc?
- were there any exceptions to the general categories of publication?
- any 'odd' publications that I could use as examples?

include Mary Walters and the 1612 funeral sermon that she wrote for herself on her deathbed

---

> *check with Dr Morton on her lecture reference to modern*
> *Virago editions*
>
> Part   • why and how did women get published?
> two?   – funeral sermons? *1630 collection as example*
>   – advice to children? *Lady Cavendish relevant enough?*
>   – pious mediations? *don't forget to include male exam-*
>   *ples for comparison*
>   – religious propaganda? *maybe have this as a section*
>   *on its own?*
>
> Part   • give examples of women in print and show how these
> three?   fit the genre

This is clearly a research sheet rather than a developed plan; it allows the student to keep an open mind as she develops her research. The first research sheet she produces might not be this organised: it might be no more than a random jotting down of ideas and sources, aimed at capturing them on paper before she thinks about the structure at all. This revised sheet shows that she is beginning to think about the structure of her work, although this will change. In the next stage of planning, she will probably decide that the 'part three' mentioned in this sheet has been superseded: she has already included all her examples in the earlier parts. You will notice that the marginal notes do not list the parts of the essay in order: as her ideas develop, she might alter these marginal notes to rearrange her material.

In the main part of the research sheet, she has listed publications that she has taken from her reading notebooks (she will add more of these in time) and she has included ideas and tasks from her research notebook. She has left plenty of space under each section of the notes so that she can add ideas as they come to her or include more notes from her reading and research notebooks. She will be using this research sheet as the basis of her work towards preparing the essay and so will study in detail the books she has mentioned, following up the references she has noted and talking to the lecturer who she remembered had given an interesting lecture on this area. She is likely to make a further research sheet or two, revising and sharpening her ideas as she works towards a final plan. When she has produced what seems to be the definitive research sheet, this can easily be developed into a plan for her assessed essay. She will include in the plan all the works she has finally decided to use; she will make a note of which ideas are her original thoughts and which are drawn from other sources; she will also include some whole sentences or paragraphs that came to her as she made her research sheets, as these will help her to remain on track with her planned ideas.

In addition to these details, she will also, crucially, include a word count for each planned section of her essay. This word count might change as she writes, but if she has an initial word count written on her plan she will not find herself in the demoralising position of finding that she has 'used up' all her allocated words in the first section of her essay and now has no words left for the next three sections. It is unlikely that she will be using too few words: postgraduates rarely find themselves in this position.

The techniques suggested in this chapter can seem like hard work because you are being asked to juggle so many tasks at one time, but if you keep updating your reading notebooks and research notebook, you will be able to review where you are from time to time and draw together disparate ideas as you progress. Having done all this, you will take control of your workload, but you might still be open to the dangers of losing track of time; time management is the final technique you will need to employ in order to succeed in your postgraduate course.

► **Time management**

Time management will vary greatly from one postgraduate course to another. If you are undertaking a fully taught course, you can expect to work within a heavily timetabled structure, with lessons and seminars, and your time management task will be one of fitting in all your coursework as you work towards examinations. On a distance or open learning course, you might have an equally well-defined structure, with deadlines for coursework and intermittent seminars or residential learning sessions to attend. In a course that is principally research-based, or in a combination taught and research course, you will be expected to juggle the demands placed upon you with your own, independent work. Whatever course you have chosen, time management is going to be crucial to your success.

The first task before you is to decide how you work best when you are studying. You might need to think back to how you worked at school or college or within your undergraduate work. Alternatively, you might draw upon your professional experience: how do you work towards deadlines? What techniques have you employed that you could reutilise now? Some postgraduates prefer to work steadily and methodically towards deadlines, others tend naturally towards a frantic last-minute push to get the work done. You will know into which category you fall, and there is no reason to assume that you will have to change your natural pattern of working now. It is easy to think that you are now a postgraduate and so must adopt a whole new way of working. In reality, whatever has worked for you in the past will serve you well now. What is certain is that, whichever working pattern you adopt, you are the only person who is going to be able to achieve the results. However supportive your lecturers, family and friends, you will have to develop, and maintain, a high level of motivation and self-discipline if you are to manage your course rather than just responding to each immediate task, with the risk of losing your overview of what you intend to achieve.

Postgraduates have to be realistic about the competing demands of home and university life. Your course will extend over at least one year, and perhaps far more than that, and it is idealistic to expect that you can keep up a total commitment to your studying, at the expense of the rest of your life, for the duration of your course. Instead you will have to take a practical approach to the situation, incorporating the demands of your life into your work programme. A postgraduate course is not, of course, an impossible journey, but you can be overwhelmed or sidetracked by your workload if you do not plan your tasks in advance. If you rely just upon the deadlines that are set for you, you will feel that you are less in control of the process than you would like. If you simply set your own deadlines, regardless of those set within your course (and a surprising number of postgraduates do just this), you will feel constantly divided, working against the expectations of your programme rather than working within them.

By far the most effective way to tackle the issue of time management is to make your own, personalised timetable. This will take into account both the way in which you naturally work best, and the demands and deadlines placed upon you by your course. The good news is that you can produce a timetable for yourself very early on in your studying, as most of the requirements of your course will be apparent within the first few weeks. It is vital that you do not put this task to one side in the hope that you will get around to doing it at some point: three months can go by in a flash and by then you will have lost valuable opportunities to make the most of your time. Naturally, each postgraduate's timetable will vary, but the timetable below will give you an idea of how it can work for you. I have taken for this example a postgraduate who is undertaking a one-year, full-time course leading to a postgraduate diploma in careers guidance. The course is taught in the first two terms, followed by the production of a 20,000 word dissertation. This is the personalised timetable that the student has produced for his second term.

	Taught work	*Assessed work*	*My tasks*	*Dissertation*
Week One	Seminar: counselling techniques. Lectures: Module 1a Module 1b		Update reading notebooks	Consider possible dissertation topic: discuss with supervisor
Week Two	Lectures: Module 1c Module 1d	Prepare for seminar presentation	Light week	
Week Three	Seminar: careers research. Lectures: Module 2a Module 2b	Give seminar presentation: assess feedback. Begin reading for first coursework	Visit central careers library – talk to advisors?	Update research notebook. Attend group discussion on planning my dissertation
Week Four	Reading week	Discuss plan for coursework with supervisor	Catch up on reading in reading notebooks. Update reading notebooks	Update research notebook. Research sheet for dissertation: will my idea work?
Week Five	Workshop: electronic databases. Lectures: Module 3a Module 3b	Continue coursework: first two sections to complete	Prepare for professional placement: find sponsor	Confirm dissertation topic: assess resources
Week Six	Guest speaker. Lecture: Module 3c	Complete coursework: deadline week seven	Update skills inventory: include tasks in timetable	Produce draft dissertation plan, including resource requirements, estimated word count and timing schedule

	Taught work	Assessed work	My tasks	Dissertation
Week Seven	Lectures: Module 4a Module 4b. Seminar: lifelong learning	Decide on group presentation topic: meet with group and arrange to rehearse in week nine	Light week	
Week Eight	Optional lecture: holistic approaches to counselling	Begin reading for second coursework. Collect evidence: questionnaire, journal search, check with sociology on theoretical underpinning. Complete written preparation for group presentation	Confirm professional placement?	Get email address of lecturer to send her plan for dissertation
Week Nine	Lectures: Module 4c Module 4d. Seminar: careers research	Prepare plan for second coursework, discuss with supervisor and begin writing. Rehearsals for group presentation	Update skills inventory: list tasks for next term's timetable	
Week Ten	Seminar: counselling techniques	Complete first section of coursework,	Visit placement provider, take	Finalise dissertation plan and list

Continued

	Taught work	Assessed work	My tasks	Dissertation
		get all material for completion over the vacation. Give group presentation	questionnaire. Prepare vacation timetable	tasks for research vacation

As you can see, our student is methodical in his approach: each task is divided and allocated a week or so of the timetable. Your timetable will be different, in that you might be more of a last-minute person, and of course your tasks will differ from those listed above, but the principles will remain the same, so it is worth looking at how this timetable will work in practice. The timetable has been divided into four sections, and in this way the student is able to see at a glance whether he is keeping up with his course requirements, and he can make adjustments within the other columns if necessary. He has included both the compulsory lectures and the optional lecture that he thinks will be of particular use to him in preparing for his dissertation.

The 'assessed work' column will have to be fairly rigidly enforced, as this term carries with it a heavy workload, but note that he is not giving an equal amount of time to each of his seminar preparations. He knows that a high percentage of his course marks is allocated to the group presentation, and he is also aware that the preparation will take longer, as there are group rehearsals to arrange and he cannot guarantee that everyone will be as well prepared as he is. He also knows that making a detailed timetable such as this will allow him to take some control of this process: when his other group members are thinking in a rather unplanned way about what they need to do, he will be able to suggest to them a timetable for completing the work that suits him best. He is making the best use of this column by making notes to himself of tasks he might otherwise forget, such as analysing the feedback from his individual presentation so that he can bear it in mind when he prepares for his group presentation. By listing the types of evidence he hopes to collect for his second coursework he will ensure that each task is completed by the time he comes to write it up.

The 'my tasks' column is vital: it is here that you will note all the tasks that are not set by your lecturers but are nevertheless essential elements in the management of your course. He has noted down two 'light weeks' here, and these are important. You cannot hope to keep up the impetus throughout the term without giving yourself some breathing space. These two weeks allow him to take stock of his course objectives and requirements, attend to domestic commitments that have built up and take a bit of a break, which everybody needs at some point. Even if you are a little behind in your planned course of work, try to keep these light weeks as clear as possible.

It may seem premature for our student to have included a column for his dissertation at this stage, but there are several reasons why this is a good idea. It will ensure that his dissertation ideas are allowed to develop as he attends seminars or lectures that might have a bearing upon it. It will give him the chance to discuss his dissertation plan with his supervisor as it develops and access resources well before he comes to write the dissertation. It will also help him to avoid the trap of finding that he has not located enough material for any work that he hopes to do on his dissertation over the vacation. The note that he must prepare a vacation timetable is also important: by making a more relaxed, but still structured vacation timetable he can ensure that he keeps on track throughout his course. In the vacation timetable he will include a mix of reading, research tasks and writing, but he will also try to include at least a week with no tasks at all. You cannot be too hard on yourself: you need some time to relax and take in what is happening to you. So many postgraduates burn themselves out in their first couple of terms that this is a serious issue for you to consider. If you take some time away from your studying and try not to allow yourself to feel guilty about it, you will be in a far better position to approach the next term with renewed enthusiasm. Although you will not be following a plan of work within this time off, you will still be doing valuable work without even realising it: you will be considering your position in relation to your subject area, mulling over undeveloped ideas and casually revisiting thoughts and connections that you have put to one side, and this is all valid work, even if you are not sitting at a desk or slaving over a hot computer.

There is one more column that you might choose to include in your personalised study timetable, one that you might entitle 'personal'. In this column you would include deadlines from your working life, if you are working as well as studying, or family holidays and special events that will impinge upon your course. You might not want to feel as if every week of your life is so highly organised that you no longer have space to breathe, but achieving a balance between home, work and study is a tricky task, and by bringing your personal commitments into your study timetable you can at least create the basis for a balanced life.

Your personalised study timetable is not intended to be a rigid plan, fixed and immovable regardless of what life, and your course, throws at you. It is a flexible scheme of work, a timetable that can be altered and expanded as more tasks are set and more deadlines imposed. You might still feel that the workload is too heavy at times, but by taking charge of it in this way you can, at the very least, see a way through your course and so continue with the challenge of managing it rather than letting it manage you.

Spot guide

Key points to remember from this chapter:

- take control of your course: manage it, rather than letting it manage you
- be an active note-taker: your initial notes are just your starting point
- develop a standard format for all your notes
- keep reading notebooks and update them periodically
- keep research notebooks and use them to the full
- look for connections everywhere: they are there, you just need to spot them
- do not shy away from exploring other disciplines occasionally
- produce research sheets for each area of research
- join discussion groups
- develop study partnerships if you can
- time management is crucial: develop strategies to master your time
- create your own timetable and use it to manage all the elements of your course

7 What if Things go Wrong?

Troubleshooting guide

Read this chapter for help in the following areas:

- if you cannot find the material you need in your university library or resource centre
- if you have missed a seminar or lecture
- if you are running out of time to complete a piece of work
- if you are running out of money
- if you are disillusioned with your course
- if you are anxious about giving a presentation or facing examinations
- if you do not enjoy your seminars
- if you feel isolated
- if you are always running out of time
- if you feel as if you are losing the plot altogether
- if you need more support for your studying
- if you feel tired all the time

This chapter might read like a litany of disasters, but that is not an accurate reflection of the postgraduate experience you will have. For most of your time you will only encounter the challenges and hurdles that you had expected to face. However, once an unexpected problem emerges, it can assume huge significance, out of all proportion to the initial difficulty. This is a natural response: however small a problem might seem to anyone else, it is your problem, it is distracting you from your work and it has to be resolved before you can move on. The aim of this chapter is to identify some of the most common difficulties that postgraduates may encounter and suggest practical solutions to them. You are likely to consult this chapter if life begins to go wrong for you, but there are two things to bear in mind as you work through it. Firstly, if you do not see your problem listed here, it does not mean that it is unique to you or too awful to be mentioned, it is simply that the experience of each postgraduate is different, throwing up individual challenges that might relate to those listed below, but not be so common as to be itemised separately. If this is the case for you, turn to the chapter that covers your general area of difficulty, as the solution to your problem will probably be found there and has not been included here simply to avoid repetition. Secondly, remember that specialised books are also available to guide you through specific problems. However, it seems a shame to spend too much time addressing a problem with a specialised guide when your difficulty might be overcome easily: most postgraduate problems are. You could use this chapter as your starting point, work with the suggestions made and then read up in more depth if the difficulty remains unresolved.

Working at postgraduate level can be an emotional seesaw. For much of the time you will be content with your course and satisfied with the results you are producing, but it is inevitable that you will occasionally feel less secure, less positive about what you are doing. This is not a problem in itself if you remember that the hurdle you are facing is most likely to be a normal part of postgraduate life. It will still need to be addressed, but there is no need to panic, thinking that you are unusual in the difficulties you face or that nobody else is encountering similar problems. Your university or college will have seen thousands of postgraduates through the process of gaining their qualifications, so all the help, advice and support you need should be available to you, if only you can find it. The whereabouts of this help will form the bulk of the guidance in this chapter.

If you are not struggling with any difficulties as your course progresses, you might still find this chapter useful. As you read about each potential problem area, you might think about how it could be relevant to you as your course develops. You might not, for example, have any problem with library catalogue searching, but you will become aware that electronic journals could also form a large part of your resources database, and mastering the search techniques required for this is a task that you might choose to take on now, before it becomes a problem. The guidance offered here is based upon common sense and experience, but common sense is not always common practice when you are anxious and even the most simple of solutions can seem obscure once your panic levels begin to rise.

You are not sure which course to take next

An odd problem to begin with, you might think; indeed, it hardly seems like a problem at all at first glance, but can become a real stumbling block. You begin on a course of study with the intention simply of completing the course and moving on with your life: this is particularly true of vocational postgraduate courses. You may then realise that this is something you do not want to give up, you are so interested in the course, and the studying and research, that you begin to see that a one-year course (or whatever) will not be enough. If you feel like this, there are some guidelines to follow:

* *Start early.* Although applying to do a further course can sometimes be left until the last minute, you will need to begin the application process early if you are to apply for funding. It will not be a disaster if you change your mind later, but it is frustrating to find that you have missed deadlines by delaying your application. If you apply early enough, your next course could have a bearing upon the work you do now: you will have your next research route in outline in your mind as you work through your current course and this will save you time and effort in the future.
* *Analyse what you enjoy most about your course.* This is vital. Is it the studying itself, almost regardless of the subject matter? Are you fascinated by the sphere of research? Are you keen to develop your academic skills beyond your current course? Can you see a career advantage in a further course?
* *Try not to rush into a decision.* Once you have analysed what is making you want to go further with your studying, there is no need to assume that you will continue with your current field of interest. Perhaps you need to embark on a purely academic course or develop just one aspect of your research into a PhD. If you rush into a further course without looking at every possible option, you will risk becoming disillusioned in the future.
* *Talk to your supervisor.* Your situation will probably come as no great surprise: your supervisor will be used to students wanting to extend their postgraduate experience beyond their initial course. You will be offered plenty of guidance as to how to move forward.

You cannot find the material you need in your university library or resource centre

In itself, this can hardly be classified as a serious problem, as it is such a common experience for all postgraduates. However, if you need to range further afield than your own university library or resources centre, you can save yourself time and trouble:

* *Use your interlibrary loan system.* If you used your library only to access fairly standard books as an undergraduate, you might be surprised at the access they have to more unusual publications. The interlibrary loan system is well developed and although there is often a charge made for

each book you borrow in this way, you might be given vouchers to offset the cost.

- *Use your supervisor.* If a book is not available within your library, and it is a principal text in your subject field and one that you might need to use for some time, it is worth checking whether your supervisor has a copy you can borrow before you order it from another library.

- *Use your library's catalogue system.* Although your library staff will help you in every way possible, it makes sense for you to locate the book if you can before you request it on the interlibrary loan system. The CD-ROMs in your library are not always well publicised, but you should be able to check the details of those books housed in the major holding libraries. There are also general CD-ROM publication catalogues that work on the basis of search terms, including the author's name, the titles of an article or book and so on, and these are useful if you have only partial information about a book or article.

- *Obtain a written reference.* It is not possible to walk into a major holding library or a university library other than your own and expect to be given access to the book that you need. You will need to obtain a written reference from your supervisor, assuring the librarians that you are trustworthy and a bona fide academic. It is a good idea to ask for this written reference some weeks before you expect to use it, so that you are ready to go once the need arises.

- *Reference libraries are not lending libraries.* This can be a real trial. You cannot take the book away, so you have to study it in the library, and you will have to order the book or article if it is not on the open shelves. You can waste hours of precious time just waiting for books to arrive on your desk. It is not uncommon to wait a whole morning for a single book, which is immensely frustrating if you have travelled some distance and only have one free day to work on the books you have selected. The answer to this problem is to prepare meticulously in advance. Make a note of all the details of a book or article and order it in advance if you can. If you do have to wait, make the most of your time by checking the library location references for other material you need or working on books that are on open access whilst you wait for the more inaccessible books. This is a great opportunity for you to update your reading notebooks, so always take them with you in case you have time to spare or find that your first choice book is not available, forcing you to rethink your plan for the day.

- *Try not to be intimidated.* It might be difficult to believe that you could be intimated by a library, but each library has its own cataloguing system, forms for ordering books and way of working; all of this carried out, of course, in hushed silence. I remember spending a ridiculous amount of time as a new postgraduate wandering nervously around a large holding library, hoping vainly for inspiration as to how to go about the supposedly simple process of obtaining a book not on the open shelves, whilst looking around at the other readers who seemed entirely at ease with the system. I was frustrated at my own ignorance and irritated at the lack of help, until I plucked up the courage to ask, firmly, for what I wanted.

- *Leave yourself enough time.* In most instances, you will be able to gain access to the material you need within a reasonable amount of time, but there will be occasions when you have to wait for a book to be returned to the library, which can disrupt your plans. The answer is to find out the availability of the publications you will need two to three weeks before you think they might become crucial to your plans and include this task in your personalised timetable.

You have missed a seminar or lecture

This happens to even the most dedicated of students and it does not have to be a major problem, as long as you cover these points:

- *Decide why you missed the event.* You might have got the timing confused, missed the bus or something equally straightforward. However, if you missed the seminar or lecture because you were drinking coffee or engrossed in some research, you need to think about why you did not attend, as there may be an underlying problem. If it is nothing more than that you are having an off day, this is no problem, but if you are finding a series of lectures boring, you might want to consider whether the subject overall is no longer inspiring you. If you have missed a seminar, is it because you find one tutor difficult to understand or you find it hard to speak up in group situations? These problems can be overcome, but you need to address them early on.
- *Contact the tutor or lecturer.* Many undergraduates seem to be capable of missing lectures and seminars with absolute ease and little concern: as a postgraduate you will be expected to take a more dedicated approach and this can bring unanticipated benefits. Just this morning a postgraduate emailed to let me know that she will be unable to attend my lecture next week. In a class of over eighty students I am unlikely to have noticed her absence straightaway, but I was so impressed that she had bothered to contact me that I replied instantly, offering to lend her several of the relevant texts and send her the handouts from the lecture. I will certainly remember her for her enthusiasm if she needs help in the future.
- *Access the material.* It is usually easy enough to get hold of handouts from missed lectures or seminars, but you need to do more than this. If

you make a copy of someone else's lecture notes, you will have the chance to find out about any additional texts that were mentioned or theories that were confirmed or questioned. If you can obtain the email address of the lecturer involved, you will still be able to get long-term help on a subject, even if you missed the initial lecture.

You will not be able to meet a course deadline

This can happen even to the keenest of students, so there is no need to feel that you have failed; you simply need to assess what has gone wrong and then get help:

- *Analyse why the work is running over time.* There are many reasons why a piece of work can take longer than expected and most of them are easily resolved. If you simply underestimated the amount of work involved, you can put this right when you come to face your next task. If you had to abandon your first hypothesis and develop another, you already know why it has taken longer than expected. However, there may be a more intractable problem. Perhaps you find taking notes from texts too time consuming? Maybe you are not revising your notes after lectures and so wasting time at the writing-up stage? Do you find it difficult to express yourself in writing? Do you spend too much time worrying about what you have been asked to do? Are you unsure about your subject area or trying to avoid one aspect of it? Is your home life impinging more than you had expected upon your studying time? It is only by deciding whether you have a fundamental problem or are simply being caught out by events in this one instance that you can decide whether you need to take long-term action to prevent the problem from happening again.
- *Talk to your supervisor.* Approach your supervisor as soon as you know that you have a timing problem. If you can arrange for an additional supervision at that stage, you will be able to talk through your plan, discuss any difficulties and reassure yourself that you are on the right lines, even if this particular piece of work is likely to take a little longer than you had planned. By arranging for an extension to the deadline for the work, if that is possible, you will be completing it under far less pressure and will not waste time worrying.
- *Revise your personalised timetable.* There are two ways in which you might have to revise your timetable if you have run over time on a piece of work. Firstly, you will want to shuffle your tasks around so as to make allowances for the time you have lost. This will stop you from working under too much pressure in the coming weeks. Secondly, and as importantly, you will need to take an overview of your plan and the time you have allowed for your tasks. Should you be leaving more space in your

timetable for each piece of coursework? Could you allow a little more time in your vacation plan for general preparation for the coursework that will come up next term? If you revise your timetable now, in the light of your current experience, you have more chance of facing the next piece of coursework in a positive frame of mind, confident that you will not overrun again.

You are running out of money

Your financial situation is necessarily unique to your circumstances. If you are in serious financial difficulty, you will need more specialist help than is offered here, but these general guidelines will help you to avoid some of the common financial problems faced by postgraduates:

- *Explore all your funding options.* This has already been mentioned, but is worth reiterating here. Even if you feel that your chances of obtaining funding are almost non-existent, take the time to make sure that you really have explored every possible funding avenue, particularly if you are intending to extend your course or move onto a further course. Hardship funds are available at many universities but are not always well publicised.
- *Make a financial plan.* Even if you do not expect to run into financial problems, it is still a good idea to make a plan, even a very basic plan, in order to control your cash flow. If you have difficulties, this plan will become a vital tool in working out where things have gone wrong; it is only by identifying your specific problems that you can hope to find a solution. This plan will not be fixed: it is better to review and revise it regularly, perhaps each month, so that you can spot any potential problems before they become a painful reality. A plan will also allow you to raise extra cash in advance of costs, with minimal disruption to your course, and alert you to the need to reschedule your debts if this becomes necessary.
- *Plan for and reduce your fixed costs.* Some costs will fluctuate during your course (mobile phone, socialising and so on) but others can be incorporated into your plan in advance (placements, specialist equipment and so on), so find out how much these costs are likely to be before you encounter them. Some fixed costs can be reduced. You know that you will need books, but study them first in the library if you can before committing to buying them, and find out whether your department or school runs a system for selling second-hand books. You will have travel costs, but these could be reduced with careful planning or by arranging lift shares. These are obvious points, but a surprising number of postgraduates overlook these basic considerations and then find that their course has cost them far more than they had expected or was necessary.

- *Minimise the cost of borrowing.* We often face our finances by lurching from one short-term solution to another. As a postgraduate you do not have to rely upon your expensive credit cards. Career development loans and relatively low interest overdrafts are a better way to tackle the problem, although these need some planning, so prepare your strategy early.
- *Try not to panic.* Easier said than done, I know, but if you can keep your head and act as soon as a financial crisis is looming, you will have time to access any hardship fund available to you, reschedule your debts or arrange top-up loans.
- *Get help.* Worrying constantly about your finances is always a major distraction in the management of your postgraduate course. You will lose valuable research and studying time thinking about the situation and you are less likely to approach those who can help you most. Your supervisor will be able to talk through the problem with you, but you can get specialist help from your welfare officer in your Students' Union or the postgraduate finance office of your university or college. If you are relying upon financial support from your partner or family, they will be horrified to be faced, out of the blue, with a stack of unexpected bills, but will be able to help if you let them know about the problems as early as possible.

You are disillusioned with your course
It can be difficult to decide why you are disillusioned with your course. All postgraduates feel less positive about their courses from time to time, but if you feel uninspired by your work, to the point where you begin to doubt you are on the right course, there are practical measures you can take to address the situation:

- *Separate out the problem.* You will have to ask yourself fundamental questions about the nature of your problem. Is the course in practice very different from what you had expected? Are you finding the work harder than you thought it would be? Is it your independent research project that is giving you unexpected difficulties? Are you struggling with the technology on your course? Are there specific tasks you find difficult? Are you beginning to doubt that the course will be relevant to your future career plans? It is only by separating out your particular area of difficulty that you can begin to work towards a solution.
- *Do not give up.* Just one problematic aspect of a course can make you feel like giving up, but this is not the solution. Instead, be proactive about your situation. You can get help with your study skills, you can alter the title of your thesis or dissertation, you can find new inspiration just by

talking through your problems. You will find it difficult to forgive yourself if you give up without a fight, however intractable the problem seems,
so make sure that you explore every possible solution.

* *Do not suffer in silence.* If you approach your supervisor with a general
feeling of disillusionment, you will get a sympathetic ear, but you need
more than that. By identifying your specific problem, you can expect a far
more productive response. If you are not enjoying one aspect of your
course, your supervisor can reassure you that the next module will be
more to your liking. If you have specific difficulties with one aspect of
your studying, your supervisor can direct you towards study skills workshops that can support you. However dreadful you feel about your
course, it is unlikely that you have made completely the wrong choice.

You are anxious about giving a presentation or facing examinations

Examinations were discussed in detail in Chapter 2 and presentations will
be explored in Chapter 9, but there are a few general tips for success:

* *You are not alone.* However interested you are in your chosen subject,
being asked to give a seminar presentation can be daunting if you have
little experience or are naturally quite shy, but you can take some comfort
from the fact that most postgraduates will feel the same way. You could,
of course, use this to your advantage. If you can find a practice partner
who shares your anxiety, you will be able to rehearse together and reassure each other as you improve your presentation skills. It is also reassuring to know that you really will get better at presenting relatively
quickly. Just an hour or two given over to practising will leave you feeling
far more positive about this challenge.

* *Get the help you need.* Too often it is assumed that postgraduates can
simply be flung into new situations and they will cope, regardless of their
past experience. This overlooks the fact that you want to do more than
just cope: you want to excel. If you fear that you will have problems with
examinations or presentations, read the relevant chapters in this book
and then follow your instincts. If you need more help, be clear about this
and ask your supervisor or departmental secretary about the courses and
workshops that are on offer to help you.

* *Master the techniques.* You might never become a natural presenter or
learn to relish the challenges of examinations, but this does not mean
that you cannot employ simple techniques that will help you to shine,
despite your natural reluctance. Be methodical in your approach and try
to see it as just another challenge on your course. Work through the
advice given in Chapters 2 and 9, safe in the knowledge that you do not

have to become 'a natural' in order to succeed: you simply have to be persistent in mastering the techniques.

You do not enjoy your seminars

The ways in which postgraduate seminars work and how you can make the most of them were discussed in Chapter 3. If you are generally happy with the seminar system, but find one of your seminar groups uninspiring or difficult, there are two points that you might consider:

- *Prepare meticulously for each seminar.* It is a truism that the more you put into seminars, the more you will get out of them. If you have studied the material you have been given thoroughly, prepared the questions you want to ask and the areas you want to explore in more detail, you will be able to make the most of each seminar. It is perfectly possible for you to skew the direction a seminar takes by preparing well in advance and being clear about your research needs. In this way seminars will become fundamental to your progress.
- *View each seminar as an individual learning opportunity.* Even if your seminar group is uninspiring, you can use this to your advantage. By having your questions and comments ready and putting all your energy into each seminar, you can draw upon the experience of your seminar tutor and feel that the seminar is addressing your particular needs. In this way you might attend seminars that simply become conversations between you and your seminar tutor. Not the ideal way to conduct a seminar, perhaps, but valuable from your point of view. Most members of the group may not have become involved, so you will not have heard their views, but you will have gained from the experience despite their apathy.

You feel isolated

A level of isolation is an integral part of a postgraduate course, in that you will be spending time working on your own ideas and research. However, when isolation begins to feel more like loneliness, you need to take action, and there are several ways to solve the problem:

- *Become active in your department.* Some people just seem to have the knack of fitting in wherever they are. You can see them in your department, chatting with the secretaries over the photocopier, having lunch with lecturers and generally looking as if they belong. If you are not that sort of person, you run the risk of feeling isolated from your department or school, especially if your timetable is quite light or your lectures are held some distance from your main department. The first thing you must do is to look around, making sure that you have checked all the notices and posters advertising events: do not assume that they are not relevant to you. Then, become involved in any discussion group available to you. Finally, attend any research seminars in your department that might interest you. Most universities have several research centres, the role of which is to bring together experts who give seminars on their latest works in progress. If there are no notices in your department about research seminars such as this, ask your supervisor to include your name on the relevant mailing lists. You will see lecturers in quite a different light at these events and your presence there will break down any barriers that you feel might exist between you.

- *Use the support structure of the university.* Universities run a wide range of support groups for undergraduates and postgraduates alike. They are not always well advertised, but they could be vital to you if you are feeling lonely and isolated, particularly if you are new to your university or the country in which you are studying. The chaplaincy is usually widely publicised and an active force in university life, offering both spiritual guidance, regular worship and pastoral support. Most universities have a helpline for students, often running a telephone counselling service and a drop-in centre. If you feel hesitant about approaching 'official' sources of support, this could be your first stop in getting help. Student welfare officers are usually based in your Students' Union and will help to support you with your housing needs, any language barriers you have and a range of special educational needs. You may automatically have been registered with a medical centre, but you do not have to wait until you are ill before you pay a visit. It is worth knowing where it is, and how it operates, before you need it; these centres sometimes offer workshops in stress management, which could be of great benefit to you as your workload increases. There will also be specialist support groups within your university; usually run by students and not always well publicised, these groups are designed to serve the needs of specific groups such as mature or overseas students.

- *Create your own support group, even before you need it.* By the time you are feeling isolated and low, it can be difficult to raise your enthusiasm to create a support group, so do it in advance. If you have a good seminar group, get into the habit of arranging to meet occasionally outside seminars to talk through your work (and moan about your workload). Make sure that your friends and family really appreciate how hard you are working and how lonely the work can sometimes make you feel. If you keep them up to date with your progress when things are going well, they will be far more responsive when you moan that things are going wrong. As suggested before, try to find a study partner (Chapter 8 will give you more details on this) so that you never become completely isolated.

- *Vary your work tasks.* Students sometimes mistake boredom for isolation. However enjoyable your subject, wading through many texts in one morning just to find a few useful references is enough to drive anyone mad and that is when you long for company, someone to take a break with whilst you bemoan your fate. This is no problem if you have a ready supply of fellow postgraduates who also need to take coffee breaks, but it can be a strain on you if they are focused on their work at that moment. By far the most effective way to combat this is to vary your tasks. This should be easy to do if you have taken the advice offered in the earlier chapters of this book. By now you will have reading notebooks and a research notebook to update, research sheets to amend and develop, a working plan on at least one piece of work and a skills inventory to hone; all this is in addition to the main tasks of each day. When you are bored with one task, there will be several more to tackle, and you will not feel bored, or isolated, you will simply move from one task to another.

You are always running out of time

In some ways, running out of time is an inherent part of a postgraduate course. After all, you could develop your work beyond your current studying – some academics will have spent their whole working lives in your area of interest – and any subject area can be expanded almost indefinitely. So there is no need to panic: feeling as if there is not enough time can be a good thing, if it is reflecting your continued interest in your research. However, there are circumstances in which you will need to take action:

- *If you know you cannot complete the course on time.* This can happen; if you come to realise that other commitments are going to make it difficult for you to complete a dissertation on time or finish the coursework within the specified period, talk to your supervisor as soon as possible. There are ways around this problem, but only if you speak up as soon as you realise that things are going badly wrong.
- *If you cannot find the time to do as much as you would like.* Go back to your personalised timetable. Is it too ambitious? Would it be possible to reduce your workload and still fulfil the fundamental requirements of your course? Could you increase your vacation workload so that you have more space in your term time schedule? If the answer to these questions if yes, then do not just struggle on regardless. Take the situation in hand and amend your timetable now, before you become demoralised; you can always add items later if your workload eases.
- *If your reading, note-taking, essay-writing or seminar preparation regularly takes too long.* You will expect to become more efficient in all these activities as your course progresses, but if you still have a sense, after

your first term, that you are spending much longer than everyone else on these routine tasks, get help before you slide behind too much. There will be a multitude of workshops within your learning support department, designed to help with every aspect of studying, so enrol now.

* *If you have missed important events.* Although you will be tempted to keep silent, try to overcome this and find out how important the event was and see if you can replicate the work elsewhere. A missed seminar will not be a disaster, a missed residential summer school might be, so make sure that you book onto another session if one is available. As with much else, if you face up to the situation, you will find that you are not alone and there are systems in place to help you to overcome the difficulty.

You feel as if you are losing the plot altogether

This can be disorientating: having worked happily for several months, you begin to feel that nothing is quite falling into place, what was clear a few weeks ago is now muddled in your mind and what seemed relatively simple is now a huge hurdle. The problem with this feeling is that it can permeate all aspects of your course, leaving you feeling demoralised about everything you are doing. Although there could be a medical cause for this feeling, such as depression, it is more likely that it is just one aspect of your course that is confusing you, and by isolating this you can fix it and move on. There are several common areas that cause this level of anxiety:

* *You may be confused by the terms or theories offered to you.* It is disconcerting to come across terms with which you are unfamiliar, or theories that are new to you, and feel that everyone else knows what is going on and you are left behind. In reality, you are not: if you are confused, other people will be too, so make a point of fixing the problem straightaway. Do not waste time looking up the terms and theories if you are already in a seminar, just ask. You may see relieved faces around you and you will be pleased that you took the plunge.

* *You find it difficult to make connections.* Try not to worry about this: it will come to you in the end. Although the importance of making connections has been discussed, it is not something that you can force and it may be some time before any occur to you. As long as you have a research notebook and are jotting down your ideas and avenues of thought, you will begin to make connections; if you find it difficult, have a brainstorming session with your colleagues to get things going. Once you have made even a few tentative connections, others will come to you far more easily.

* *Everyone seems to be better informed than you.* Some postgraduates seem to know, as if by instinct, exactly when each seminar is to be held,

the deadlines for each piece of work and the details of every discussion group or guest speaker session being held. Others are not that organised; if you fall into this category, you can prevent it from being a problem. Make sure that your personalised timetable includes all the information you are likely to forget and then refer to it each day. If you can find an organised friend who will help you out, make the most of the opportunity by striking a deal. I once taught a student who was brilliant at all things academic, but could not get through the day without meeting up with her more organised colleague each morning to check on what had to be done. When I quizzed her friend about this, she explained to me that it was no problem for her to organise her friend, as it came quite naturally to her to know what she was doing each day and she was happy to share her knowledge; in exchange her less organised friend had agreed to chair all their meetings when they prepared for seminar presentations, as she worked better under pressure and in group situations. The trade-off worked well for them both.

- *Your research work has become confusing.* It is worth dispelling here the myth that you should be organised at all times, entirely focused on a hypothesis that you know will work and working only within the parameters you set for yourself at the outset of your course. Not only is this unrealistic, it can be positively unproductive in the case of postgraduate study. If your early ideas seem unstructured, this is all part of the learning process, a positive aspect of study. If you have no clear idea of your dissertation title or your plan keeps changing, this is also a natural part of postgraduate study, allowing you to remain creative and resourceful in your work. You can be sure that your supervisor will tell you if you need to firm up your ideas or concentrate upon one area of study. It is far more likely that you will be told to think widely, lose some of your rigid and restrictive focus, than that you will be urged to think more narrowly. If your initial hypothesis is not working, this simply means that you are working towards a more viable hypothesis and you will get there in the end, however painful the process can seem at times. Similarly, if you have spent time working on material that now seems irrelevant to your central research objective, there is no need to worry. You will not have spent too long before you decided to change tack, and work carried out that is not directly relevant can still provide extremely useful underpinning to the points you are trying to make. Although it can be frustrating, and at times worrying, to feel that things are out of control, the secret is to try not to worry too much: your supervisor will help you and your personalised timetable and research sheets will ensure that you cannot stray too far from your principal tasks before alarm bells start ringing.

You need more support for your studying

The problem of isolation has already been tackled in this chapter, but there is another relatively common problem that can feel similar but is in fact far more specific. It is the feeling you get when you no longer feel connected to, and supported by, the system. There are several ways in which this can happen, and the answer to the problem is usually quite simple:

- *You are disappointed with the feedback on a piece of work.* This can be difficult because the first person you would normally go to with your problems, your supervisor, may be the person who has given you the feedback. There are three ways to cope with this. Firstly, make sure that you understand the feedback clearly, if necessary by emailing the marker to ask for a more detailed explanation of how the mark was reached or why certain comments were made on the work. Secondly, discuss the mark with a colleague with whom you feel comfortable: it is possible that your work was marked by a lecturer who is known for harsh marking or has a bias in a direction that is opposed to the thrust of your hypothesis. You will not be able to dismiss the mark, but you will be able to view the situation in a fresher perspective. Thirdly, be brave about the situation. If you feel awful because you have received a surprisingly low mark, force yourself to think it through in depth. In calm retrospect, away from your initial disappointment, did you work on a hypothesis that did not work? The next one will. Did you overlook some vital data? You will not do that again. Did your style let you down? You can get help with this. Did you rush into making generalised statements with little supporting evidence? You are unlikely to fall into that trap a second time. Once you have identified the root of the problem, you can begin to work towards a solution, and what was a painful and distracting experience can transform itself into a valuable learning opportunity: this really is possible, however depressed you feel when you first receive a disappointing mark or confusing feedback.
- *You feel that you need more supervision.* Before you begin to regret your choice of supervisor, try to analyse why you feel this way. If you are having trouble with specific study skills, it might be a more efficient use of your time to enrol in study sessions and workshops rather than relying solely upon your supervisions. If you find that your supervisor is rarely in the department at the right time for you, simply increase your email correspondence so that you can gain support in that way. If you are having trouble with your finances, housing or juggling your life and studying, and your supervisor is not a great deal of help, try not to assume that this is a lack of concern. It might simply be inexperience, and your best option is to make use of the specialist housing, finance

and welfare services within your university and then let your supervisor know what is going on, rather than letting these problems sour your relationship. If you have been proactive about the situation and followed these suggestions but still feel that you need more hands-on support, there are other ways around the problem, such as study partnerships, discussion groups and study support groups, but first try telling your supervisor how you feel. Perhaps you look so organised and in control of your life that it has never occurred to your supervisor that you needed more time together. Even if your supervisor tends not to offer plentiful supervisions, it should be possible to arrange for an increased number of sessions for a time.

You feel that you are failing

This problem can hit you unexpectedly and have a disastrous effect on the management of your course unless you tackle it as soon as it arises. One poor mark does not indicate that you are not achieving well enough on every section of your course, and you can follow the advice offered above in order to cope with your natural feeling of disappointment. If you have failed an assessed part of your course, perhaps a module examination or a presentation, or if you are concerned that you might be on the road to failing the course in its entirety, there are steps you can take:

- *Understand the assessment procedure.* It is not always made clear to postgraduate students whether one fail mark will exclude them from the possibility of passing their course as a whole. They are also sometimes uncertain as to whether a mark given to them is actually a fail mark. Forty per cent might, for example, be an acceptable mark for a piece of coursework and yet represent a fail grade for a presentation. Before you assume that you have failed, make sure that you know how the assessment works for each aspect of your course.
- *Calculate how important this failure is to your overall course.* You will be disappointed in any fail mark, but there are occasions where one fail mark is allowable and will not disqualify you from completing your course successfully. It is essential that you understand how the assessment system works before you assume the worst.
- *Be clear about the reassessment.* Assessment is rarely as inflexible as you might suppose. Nobody is going to change your mark simply because you are disappointed to have received it, but there will be systems in place to allow you to resit examinations or resubmit assessed pieces of work. Even if you are at the stage of sitting a viva for your final dissertation or thesis, you will still not be faced with a simple pass or fail situation. Your

work might be referred for amendments, and this will allow you time to revise specific aspects of it. It would be counterproductive to spend too much time working through all the possibilities for revision and referral if you are not failing on your course, but it is reassuring to know that such provisions exist.

* *Talk to your lecturers.* You will know, in most cases, if you are falling below the standard expected in one section of your course, and the best people to help are the lecturers who are working with you on that topic. Getting specialist guidance can solve problems before they become intractable, so be proactive about seeking help. There will also be more general support offered within your college or university: study workshops, pre-sentation courses and research discusssion groups. If you panic and get involved in each of these, regardless of your specific problem, you are likely to disrupt your personalised timetable, so pinpoint your problem first and then get the help you need.

* *Enlist the help of your supervisor.* This is perhaps the greatest test for this relationship. Your supervisor can help in a multitude of ways, from working with you through a revised plan of your work, to pointing you towards specialist groups that can help you with specific problems. Perhaps the greatest help of all is simply to be available to talk through your feelings and help you to be clear about the problem you are facing. Nothing that you say is going to faze your supervisor, but you must be honest. If you put a brave face on it, brush aside your problems and cover up your true anxieties, your supervisor will not be able to help, so be open to the guidance being offered and be clear about your perspective on how things are going wrong. In this way you can work more quickly towards a solution.

You feel tired all the time

A simple but common problem that may not be a disaster in itself, but can raise difficulties far beyond its initial importance. We are all used to living and working at a fast pace and balancing all the competing demands of our lives, but if you are tired you can feel stressed at the smallest problem and are unlikely to have the energy to work out solutions. Postgraduate life is demanding, and as a result even the most organised students can overlook the fact that they need to take care of themselves, by eating and sleeping well and, most importantly, by giving themselves a break from time to time. Your personalised timetable will help you to remain in control of your life and this will reduce your stress level, but if you feel exhausted all the time, do not overlook the possibility that the cause might be physical. Similarly, if you believe that you have identified a problem, pause for a moment before you begin to work through the suggestions offered here and ask yourself whether the root problem is not so specific, but in fact stems from lack of sleep or the fact that you are so engrossed in your course that you keep forgetting to eat lunch. Simple, I know, but very common.

This chapter has covered many of the problems that postgraduates can face from time to time. As you can see, most of them can be resolved fairly swiftly; usually identifying a problem takes you halfway to solving it. This is likely to be the chapter that you dip into from time to time as difficult issues arise. I hope it is not somewhere you will need to linger for very long before you can resolve the problem and return to enjoying your course.

Spot guide

Key points to remember from this chapter:

- look after your physical welfare
- address your problems before they build up
- identify the root cause of the problem before you feel too demoralised
- use the support services that exist within your university
- create your own support systems, tailored to your needs
- use your personalised timetable to keep on track
- try not to suffer in silence
- work with your supervisor to resolve problems
- never assume that you are alone in the difficulties you are experiencing
- be proactive by tackling issues as they arise
- never give up: there will be a solution to your problems

---

8 Teamwork and Networking

Troubleshooting guide

Read this chapter for help in the following areas:

- if you find it difficult to recognise the various teams within which you are working
- if you are not a natural team player
- if you feel isolated
- if you need more support for your studying and research
- if you are unhappy with a team within which you have been placed
- if you find it hard to speak out in group situations
- if you tend to become aggressive or dominating within a team
- if you want to make the most of your teams
- if you recognise the need to network, but are not sure how to begin
- if you feel excluded from team activities
- if you feel pressurised into team activities that are not helping you
- if you are enjoying a team and want to know how to develop it
- if you have not been offered team support for revision or presentation preparation
- if you find it difficult to dovetail your work and university life
- if you need specialist help that your supervisor cannot offer you
- if you feel that your family and friends do not understand what you are going through
- if you prefer to work in a one-to-one study situation

Becoming part of a team and learning how to network effectively will not, perhaps, be the first aspects of managing your postgraduate course that you will consider. After all, you know that much of your time will be spent in the solitary pursuit of research material or working out the best way to present your ideas, so teamwork and networking might be low on your list of priorities. However, there are two good reasons to give them a higher priority, once you have mastered the fundamentals of postgraduate study. Firstly, and rather pragmatically, employers need team players. It is relatively cheap to retrain staff or allow them time in which to develop the required skills, but if they cannot become part of a team, the problem is more intractable. If employers take a stereotypical view of a postgraduate as having spent a year or more sitting in a library carrying out research, with little interaction with other people, it is going to be your task to change their minds. To do this you will need to have analysed the teamwork that has been part of your postgraduate experience, so that you can sell the idea that you are a team player, able to fit into a professional team as easily as you fitted into your postgraduate teams.

The second, and at this stage more important, reason for you to make the most of the teamwork and networking that are part of your course is that teams can offer you essential support. If these aspects of your course are mishandled, you risk not only losing out on this support, but also becoming distracted from your primary purpose. If you have identified the teams of which you form part, and decided how to get the best value from them, you will be able to get help when you need it and create a support structure that will last for the duration of your course. There are several teams with which you might be involved during your postgraduate course:

- seminar/class teams
- research teams
- presentation teams
- department/university teams
- supervisor/supervisee teams
- occasional teams
- work teams
- social teams
- support teams
- study partnerships.

Before I move on to consider these teams individually, it is worth spending a little time considering how you might maximise the benefits of any team situation.

▶ Analysing a team

It can be counterproductive to work in a team without having understood how it is intended to work, what purpose it is hoping to serve and how you are expected to fit into it, so considering these factors is going to be necessary for success.

Do you have a choice?

If you are part of a professional team, you will have little choice as to the selection of the other members of your team. Similarly, undergraduates tend to be placed in teams in which they are required to work. As a postgraduate, you may have some choice. Although you will want to be a constructive member of the team, helping others with their studying and research, you will not want to waste time struggling with a team that is offering you little in return for all your efforts. If you are really not enjoying working in a particular team, finding it hard to communicate with the other members or feeling that they are not as dedicated as you, do not waste too much time in frustrated efforts to make the team work. If you have tried all the suggestions below and really feel that there is no hope, find out if you can be moved to a team which is more in tune with your ways of working.

How large is the team?

This may seem obvious, but academic teams tend to grow without planning; a study group that opens with three members may grow to four times that number as other students become aware of its value or change their course options. You need to be alert to this possibility because it can be disconcerting to find that your comfortable team of three has expanded to a dozen without anyone considering how this will affect the overall working of the group. If this happens to you, be aware of the potential difficulties, and if you find that a larger team precludes you from working in ways that united you in the past, decide whether the team is divisible for at least part of the time that you are studying together or make a conscious effort to devise new methods of working that suit your new situation.

Is there a history to the team?

This can be one of the most insidious problems within academic teams. You are asked to join a seminar group, become part of a team organising a conference or organise a discussion group. In your enthusiasm, you might overlook the fact that the seminar group has been in existence for three months and has its own unique way of working, last year's conference was a disaster or another student desperately wanted to organise the discussion group but was not asked. It need not be difficult to check the history of your team, but make sure that you avoid lurking problems by doing it as early as possible.

How can we communicate?

Your first task is to work out whether the team members have worked together before, whether they all recognise each other and whether there is any obvious reason why the team might encounter difficulties. You then need to ensure that you can communicate effectively as a team. This may be no more than a matter of exchanging email addresses, but do not assume that anyone will think of this for you. Lecturers are quite happy to see their teams periodically and presume that they have worked out how best to work together in the interim, so take it upon yourself to establish effective lines of communication at the outset. There are times when email is not enough: do not ignore the benefits of meeting with your team so that ideas can be exchanged more freely and plans developed face to face. The most effective teams tend be those that vary their approach to communication, tailoring the means of communication to each new task.

Your contribution

At a basic level your contribution is clear: you are a member of a team so that you can support the work of others whilst benefiting from the team's activities yourself. However, this can only work if you have asked yourself the fundamental question: why does this team exist? This involves not only looking at the tasks given to the team (a seminar group exists to explore ideas, a discussion group offers wider support, an organisational group is created to arrange an event and so on) but also considering the wider objectives involved (a seminar group might also provide a long-term network system, a discussion group might bring lecturers and students together in a social setting, an organisational group might be expected to support new teams and so on). You will have your own way of contributing to any team and you need to analyse now how best you work within a team. Are you a natural leader? Do you prefer to support the team's work, rather than leading it? Do you find speaking out in groups difficult? If you know the team's aims and understand the wider objectives, you will be in a strong position to reap the benefits of the teamwork in which you are taking part.

Do personalities matter?

The simple answer to this is 'yes'. There is no point in assuming that, because you have identified realistic aims and recognisable objectives, you will get along with each other. It would be unusual if you liked every member of all your teams equally and never found yourself disagreeing with team members. Do not spend time worrying about this or fretting about what you see as the inadequacies of another team member. Instead, play to your strengths within the team and work hard to overcome any problems. If, for example, one member dominates every meeting, suggest that you take turns in giving short presentations at team meetings, so that everyone has the chance to express themselves. If you find that a team discussion never really gets going, you might suggest that some of the preliminary work is carried out by email. If, in your opinion, a team member has a difficult personality, structure meetings in such a way that conflict is minimised.

Planning for success

Whatever the personalities involved in a team, you can keep things on schedule and maintain the productivity of the team by remembering that teams always work at their best if they achieve the following:

* *cooperation*: the onus is on each member of the team to create this
* *allocation of tasks*: each team member needs to be clear about each task
* *communication*: be creative about how to achieve this
* *realism*: try to avoid stretching the team too thinly over a wide range of tasks
* *focus*: confirm your plans in writing so that each person remains on task
* *clarity*: this is often achieved by taking minutes of even informal meetings
* *perspective*: clear aims and objectives at each stage will be vital
* *linkage*: each team member's contribution must fit into the overall task
* *decisive action*: you do not have the time to spend on meetings that go nowhere
* *measurable results*: every team needs to know where it is going and when it has got there.

Understanding team dynamics

There is not always enough time for you to get to know each member of your team well before you are asked to deliver results, so you will need to have assessed your own strengths as a team player in advance and be ready to use them. You might also consider carrying out a formal skills analysis within the team in its early stages. This can sound intimidating, but need not be. When you first meet as a team, part of the process of getting to know each other could involve asking team members to give details of their areas of interest and some background information concerning their team experiences and relevant skills. If they are asked to think about this before a meeting, they will have time to prepare and the team will not risk overlooking talents that it needs.

Remain aware of the outside world

Although your principal focus will be upon the team and its work, it makes sense to remain aware of the wider implications of your teamwork. If you are arranging an event, you will have the opportunity to network beyond your initial team. If you are working as part of a research team, you are in the ideal position to identify other teams working in your area with which you might like to be involved in the future. One team tends to lead to another, so make sure that you find out what other teams your fellow team members are involved in, in case they could be of use to you as your course progresses. As a project draws to a close, it is essential that you consider your future:

could your current research team prepare a credible bid for additional funding? Could your seminar team act as a networking group as you all search for jobs? Could your discussion group meet to discuss career opportunities? Could your study group be transformed into a presentation or revision group? It is surprisingly easy to lose all sight of the outside world as you work towards your team goals but this will be to your detriment, so try to avoid it happening to you.

Time management

You may already have strong time management skills and so be able bring your personalised timetable to bear on group activities, arranging rehearsals for group presentations at times that suit you or holding meetings during your 'light' study weeks. The key to effective teams is to identify the timescale within which you will be working. You will not want to spend a disproportionate amount of time working with a team for a group presentation to the detriment of a more long-standing study team, nor will you want to cut down on the time you give to your seminar teams. Most of your colleagues will not have given much thought to the overall time management involved in their courses, so you can make the most of your own higher level of organisation. Although you will have established a time frame at the outset, make sure that you review the timescale periodically and allocate set times, if you can, to various activities, such as the length of meetings, the amount of time to be taken for each task and the ways in which you can maximise the time available. Altering meeting structures can save time (you might, for example, ask one member to present an overview of the current situation rather than just talking around the subject) as can the regular use of emails to disseminate information. You might have to make compromises on timing as events develop, but knowing that you are going to run out of time before you hit crisis point will allow the group as a whole to work towards a solution.

Becoming assertive

Being an assertive team member is *not* the same as being an aggressive team member. You might be able to impose your personality upon your team members, insisting that they work to your timetable, using your working methods and achieving the goals you have set. However, if you did this you might have to ask yourself whether you are actually working as part of a team or simply working on your own in a room where other people happen to be sitting. You might achieve your goals (although this is not guaranteed), but you will have missed the opportunity to work in a supportive team and might have caused so much resentment that the team experience will ultimately have been counterproductive. However lethargic or disorganised other team members seem to be, you are in a team for a reason and you need to learn to be an assertive member of your team without taking it over. On the other hand, if you are too submissive within a team, you will lose the chance to become fully involved with the team effort and you might begin to resent other team members, feeling that you have not had your say or been allowed to guide events as the work develops. The secret is to learn to be assertive whilst avoiding becoming aggressive and this takes practice. If you know that this will be a problem for you, there are more detailed guides that might help you, but for most postgraduates it is enough simply to follow these guidelines:

* aim for a situation where everyone wins, allowing for reasonable compromise
* recognise and master your instinctive negative behaviour, such as avoiding conflict or bullying others
* identify the expectations of the group: can they be met?
* avoid the pressure that results from poor time management: this can increase aggression
* ask for help when you need it: a team is not a test of strength
* listen actively to each contribution to discussions
* show that you have understood what team members have to contribute: reassure them
* say what you think and feel, but only in the light of what is relevant to the current situation
* say clearly (and repeat if necessary) what you would like to happen and why
* before you reach a decision, consider the consequences for each team member and the task
* once a decision has been reached, make sure that everyone is clear about the way ahead
* keep the lines of communication open as the work develops
* be firm about sticking to the group decision
* be prepared to offer alternatives if you cannot do exactly what the group would like you to do.

▶ Identifying your teams

By examining each potential team in which you will be working, you will be able to move forward with a more positive attitude towards the teams and networks that will support you during your course.

Seminar/class teams

These teams may last for the duration of your course, so you must ensure that you get the greatest possible support from them. Making the most of seminars has already been discussed in Chapter 3, but try not to overlook the fact that, whatever your individual contribution to each seminar, it is still designed to be a team. To benefit fully from these groups, you might like to consider extending your time together beyond the timetabled seminars. This is particularly beneficial as examinations or assessments draw near. There are guidelines that you can follow in order to enjoy the advantages of these groups to the full:

• extend your meetings: meeting before or after seminars to talk through the issues raised will help to reinforce your understanding and expand your ideas
• keep in touch: you will not necessarily be given the email addresses of the other members of your seminar group, so make sure that you exchange addresses amongst yourselves
• draw upon the experience around you: if you have to give a group presentation or want to work with others as you rehearse for an individual presentation, look first to your seminar group for presentation or revision partners
• increase the long-term benefits: even if a seminar group is short-lived, you can make a positive effort to remain in contact in order to gain additional help in the future
• make it work: if you are in a class or lecture group, it might be difficult to talk at length during classes, so arrange to get together away from the lecture room.

Research teams

If you are working on a long-term project as part of a research team, you will be able to use the advice offered in the earlier sections of this chapter in order to maximise the benefits you can derive from the team. If you are part of a short-term research team, perhaps brought together for just a few weeks to investigate one aspect of your subject or evaluate a hypothesis, there is additional work to be done:

• be clear not only about the task before you, but also about the wider objectives of the team
• should you accept the task as it stands, are you clear about what is involved?
• is there a precedent for this work? Can you use the output and working methods of similar teams?
• can you achieve the objective? Discuss any obvious area of difficulty in achieving the objective as early as possible

- decide upon your own minimum goal: what do you intend to achieve in the time available?
- ensure that the whole team is aware of the plan as it develops
- work assertively with the team, planning your timetable and playing to your strengths
- keep the lines of communication open: avoid excluding any member of the team
- make sure that everyone involved in the team (and the wider academic world) is made aware of your success as the project draws to a close.

Presentation teams

You might be asked to give a presentation as part of a team, perhaps a joint research presentation or a seminar presentation. There are other circumstances in which you might present as part of a team, such as a departmental presentation to new students or a professional-level presentation at a conference. Whatever the circumstances, there are several guidelines that will always apply:

- decide how much you can cover in the time available and then cut it down. There is a natural tendency to try to include too much material in a presentation, so try at the outset to focus on a smaller area that you can handle well rather than taking on too much for the time available
- allocate speaker positions early: it is not usually a good idea to put your least confident speaker first, unless you can get away with having that speaker simply introduce the group and then sit down to let the more confident speakers take over
- be clear about the assessment system: you are most unlikely to be given individual marks for a team presentation. If you are to be marked as a team, you must work as a team
- keep in touch: exchange email addresses or contact numbers and keep updating each other regularly on your progress
- always leave time to rehearse together. An experienced assessor will know if a group has not spent time working through a presentation together, so it is essential that you rehearse as a group to polish your performance
- be ready for last-minute disasters. If one member of your team fails to arrive on the day, you are unlikely to be given an alternative date on which to present. It is essential that you can give the presentation with one member missing, so make sure that you all know the presentation well enough to rework it at the last moment or all have copies of everyone's prompt cards or notes so that you can stand in for each other. Have backup visual aids so that the presentation can go ahead regardless of last-minute technical problems.

Department/university teams

You are part of a wider team within your university, even if most of your time is spent dashing in and out of your department, attending occasional lectures or meeting with your supervisor. Although the guidance in earlier chapters will help you here, there are several key points to remember as you work within this team:

* think beyond your immediate tasks: time spent working with disucsssion groups or revising with designated study groups will prevent you from becoming isolated
* look around you: if you have come to university to do more than simply gain a qualification, you need to consider your options as early as possible, before time runs out. If you want to get involved in student groups, write for the student newspaper or become a student counsellor, the initial approach needs to be made as soon as you have settled into your course and created your individual study timetable
* be proactive: university and college departments respect the fact that some postgraduates have little time or inclination to become involved in university life beyond the parameters of their courses, so additional activities are not always well publicised: you will need to make the first move
* study widely: if you have the time, find out about other learning opportunities, extracurricular classes and university-wide conferences or seminars. The university newsletter or newspaper will publicise these events, so become as informed as possible and decide, in the early stages of your course, how much time you can realistically devote to activities beyond your basic course requirements.

Supervisor/supervisee teams

Chapter 5 was devoted to the relationship that you will develop with your supervisor, but you can think beyond this to the wider opportunities available to you:

* *research panels*: these are likely to exist within your department or school and usually only become visible to you if you are asked to give a formal presentation upon the progress of your research. Their aim is to support the research of their department, so make use of them if you need to. If you would find it useful to present your ideas earlier than is usual, knowing that you will get feedback on methodologies and research paths, ask if you can meet with them earlier and perhaps more frequently.
* *research groups*: some supervisors run research groups for their super- visees in order to discuss general research issues. If you hear of such

a group run by a supervisor other than your own, there is no need to feel that it would be disloyal to your supervisor to join the group.

* *secondary supervisors*: your supervisor might choose to call upon the expertise of other academics in supporting one aspect of your research, but if you know of an academic with whom you work well and whom you feel could help you, ask your supervisor whether it is possible to extend your supervision for a time beyond the scope of just one supervisor.
* *earlier supervisors*: you will have moved some way by now from your earlier courses of study, but there is no reason why you should not return to the supervisor who helped you through your undergraduate dissertation, or an earlier postgraduate course, for help with new challenges as they arise. This will not replace the work you are undertaking with your current supervisor but it can enhance the level of supervision you are receiving. Just one word of warning: your supervisor will not be concerned about the situation as long as you are clear about what you are doing and why you are doing it.

Occasional teams

These teams arise far more often than postgraduates usually expect. You might be asked to join a presentation team or attend a series of general lectures that are open to postgraduates across several departments or schools. You might assume that these teams will have little impact upon your course as a whole, but they can be extremely valuable because they give you the chance to work with postgraduates from other disciplines and find like-minded students with whom you can work in the future. So as to make the best of these opportunities, be proactive in your approach:

* discover how these teams are relevant to your needs: consider the wider objectives of the teams rather than focusing solely on the task before you
* include these teams in your personalised timetable: if you do not do this, they will always be a nuisance. If you have dedicated a reasonable amount of time to working within each occasional team that arises, you will be in a position to get the best from the situation
* take control of the communication: if you can find out how best you can communicate within the team (by meeting regularly or by email, for example) you will reduce the amount of time that is potentially wasted within these team situations
* continue beyond the initial task: if you work well with a particular team, do not disband the team once the initial objective has been achieved. Consider how you might work together in the future and keep in touch via email with those team members with whom you worked best.

Work teams

If you are working to support yourself financially whilst you study, or if your course is part time and vocational and thus part of your working life, it is counterproductive to presume that your work teams and your study life are entirely divorced from each other. It is better to incorporate your work team into your experience as a postgraduate, and you can do this relatively easily:

- your work colleagues may not understand your course and its requirements: even if you are studying with the full cooperation of your employer, it will still be necessary for you to give your colleagues the chance to become involved. If they are clear about the demands your course is placing upon you, and understand how it might impact upon your workload and ways of working, they will be supportive. If they have no idea of what you are doing and how you hope to do it, they will have no chance to offer you relevant and timely support.

- enhance your skills inventory: your paid work may be no more to you than a means of earning some cash whilst you study, but if you analyse it you may find that your experiences in one sphere of your life can help you to meet the demands of another. Your skills inventory need not rely solely upon your life at university or college: your paid work will also play its part in the development of an impressive skills portfolio.

- time management: employers will only be in a position to help as your course develops if they understand your timing. If you have a realistic personalised timetable, you may be able to negotiate your hours to suit your study needs. Never assume that this is not possible: even if you work for a large organisation, you might be surprised at how flexible and supportive it can become, as long as you are clear about your needs and prepared to work with them to meet their needs as well as your own.

Social teams

Some of your social teams will, of course, exist without any conscious effort on your part. You will already have a social life and university will offer you the chance to increase this, but you could now view your social life as a series of teams, each of which might be able to help you in your course:

- *existing social teams*: a good excuse to escape from work and remind yourself of what life was like before you had so much studying and research to do.

- *formal social teams*: within university, these are usually created when you join a student society or other university organisation, such as a sports club. These societies will widen your horizons and allow you to talk through the experience of being at university with others in a similar situation, but they can take up so much of your time that your formal work suffers. These groups are often led by dedicated students who spend vast amounts of time organising the group: be clear about the amount of time that you can devote to the group and use your personalised timetable to check that you are not spending too much time focusing on these groups.

* *casual social teams*: the most unlikely teams are created at university. It would not be unusual for you to form friendships with undergraduates, postgraduates from other departments or schools and lecturers. This is always a good thing, but try not to overlook the wider academic possibilities open to you within these teams. Revision groups, academic discussion groups and general study groups can form from these casual groupings and they work well precisely because you all have a different outlook and set of experiences to draw upon. As with all teamwork, the secret is to recognise that a team exists, however tenuous its origins, and it can be of use to you.

Support teams

Support teams comprise those people who are not directly involved with your course, but nevertheless offer vital financial, emotional or practical help. Although your principal support team is likely to be made up of your family and friends, there are other support teams that you might come to rely upon at various points in your course:

* *networking teams*: if you attend conferences, or take part in study or discussion groups, you will soon develop a network of academics whom you may never meet again in person, but with whom you can keep in touch by email. Never miss the opportunity to extend this team: a full email address book, with the details of the research interests of each member, can save you hours as you work through your research tasks.
* *practical teams*: the importance of these teams should not be underestimated. Although they can be fundamental to the successful management of your course, it is easy to ignore the need to organise them. If, for example, you need help with the cost of travelling, advertise as widely as possible that you would like to become involved in lift shares. If you have to miss a lecture, make sure that you have made a firm, and reciprocal, arrangement with a colleague who is happy to share lecture notes with you. In these circumstances, choose the best person for the task rather than just relying on a good friend. You need clear, detailed lecture notes and you must be sure that you can rely on the colleague to attend any lecture you have to miss. If you are living near your university or college and need to share accommodation costs, try not to rely unthinkingly

upon casual friendships to form the basis of a house share. Instead, think through the situation: are your friends really the best people with whom to share a house? Are they reliable, reasonably keen to work and capable of paying the rent? These may sound like simple considerations, but the practical teams you create will underpin everything you are trying to achieve and if they are neglected they can cause huge problems.

* *financial teams*: you will have a plan in place before you begin your course and you will update your plans as new expenses arise, but try to keep an open mind about your finances. If your principal financial backers cannot stretch their support any further, your savings are running too low or your credit cards are running too high, you will need to think as widely as possible about additional sources of support. Chapter 7 offers help in this area, so work through the options outlined there before you face a serious financial crisis.

* *emotional teams*: although you will already have a team of people who are keen to support you (even if you do not instinctively think of them as a team in this way), you can guarantee the best possible support only if you target your requests for help. A friend who has little knowledge of your course, or university life in general, may find it difficult to appreciate what you are going through academically, but might be able offer just the right level of support if your problems are financial. Family members might be so concerned about your workload and the fact that you look tired that they cannot get beyond this to help you to find solutions to your study problems. This is not a complex issue, but you do need to address it before you face each new set of challenges: if you can consider each member of your emotional support team in the light of the problem you are facing, you can be sure of receiving far more relevant and practical support.

Study partnerships

These have already been mentioned in earlier chapters and it is vital that you recognise and foster this relationship. It will consist of only two or three of you, each of whom has found that you work well together and can be of great benefit to each other. These groups will not form for everyone and many postgraduates go through university without forming such a team, but if you do discover that you work particularly well with another student, who is on your wavelength and approaches study situations in the same way as you or in a way that complements your efforts, it is worth nurturing the relationship. Your study partner might not be studying the same subject as you: it is more about a way of working than the course you are taking. It could be, for example, that you like to carry out your research in absolute quiet for long periods at a time, but prefer to have some company whilst you do it, or you enjoy talking through the framework of an assignment before you commit a plan to paper. In both cases, having a study partner or couple who are studying a different subject from you can be a positive benefit. You will work quietly for a time and then take a break together, when you will either ignore the work you have done and give your minds a rest or discuss your research, each of you asking general research questions of the others. If you are preparing your dissertation or thesis, you can discuss the plan in outline terms, even if your study partners have no direct experience of your area of interest. It is often the case that someone not concerned with your subject will ask the one fundamental question that you have failed to address or will ask you to explain a point that you had assumed was self-explanatory. You need to ensure that the trade-off works and that everyone involved gets the chance to talk, but you will find that this grouping is amongst the most productive that you will make during your postgraduate course.

Spot guide

Key points to remember from this chapter:

- you are surrounded by teams: make the most of them
- once you have identified a team, analyse its strengths and weaknesses
- always understand your team task and recognise your wider objectives
- take some control of the size, nature and working methods of your team
- identify the unique contribution that you can make to each team
- save time by varying your meeting structures and allocating tasks
- successful teams need clear objectives and a realistic time frame
- learn to be assertive in team situations
- always remain aware of the demands on your time
- keep lines of communication open
- one team leads to another: learn to network
- communication is key: always exchange email addresses
- adapt successful teams to help you in facing new challenges
- use what you learn in one team to help support you in other teams
- try to create a study partnership

---

9 Presenting your Ideas

Troubleshooting guide

Read this chapter for help in the following areas:

- if you are asked to give a research presentation
- if you are preparing to give a seminar presentation
- if you have to give a group presentation
- if you are considering writing a conference paper
- if you would like to publish your work
- if you are unsure how to fit presentation tasks into your person-alised timetable
- if you are nervous about giving presentations
- if you have trouble making your points convincingly in presentations
- if you are running out of time in your personalised timetable
- if you would like to benefit from more input into your research
- if you intend to apply for a further course
- if you are hoping to pursue an academic career

Whilst you are a postgraduate you will naturally channel your energies into producing the work that is an integral part of your course and its assessment: coursework, assessed pieces, project reports and a more extensive research project. What you might not be expecting at the outset are the additional ways in which you might be asked to present your ideas, involving work that is not part of your overall assessment but which might, nevertheless, be crucial to the successful management of your course. Courses will differ greatly in their requirements, but you need to consider four important additional ways of presenting your ideas, particularly if you are considering a career in your chosen field:

- research presentations
- seminar presentations
- conference papers
- publication.

You might not receive extensive support or instruction in how to prepare and present your ideas in these different formats. You might also feel that these tasks are a burden, getting in the way of your research plans and putting you under pressure for little return on your efforts. For both of these reasons, it is necessary to explore in some detail why they are important, how you can master them and how best to maximise the benefits to you as you manage your course.

▶ Research presentations

What is involved?

These were mentioned in Chapter 8 and often come as a shock to post-graduates. They can range in nature from formal occasions, held perhaps once or twice during your course, during which you are expected to present your work in progress and map out the future direction of your research, to more frequent, less formal meetings in which you are expected to discuss your current research tasks and your future plans. Both types of presentation will be given not just to your supervisor, but also to at least one other academic (and more usually to a research panel), and this is what makes them so much more demanding, and potentially so much more rewarding, than your everyday supervisions.

Why give them?

You will not be given an option about them, but you do have a choice about their delivery. You can either crash through them in the shortest time possible, giving away only the outline of your research and longing for the event to come to an end, or you can make a positive choice by deciding that this is being undertaken for your benefit, so you will get the most out of it. This is particularly true if you are giving a research presentation on just one aspect of your research, perhaps in preparation for a piece of assessed coursework. Whilst your supervisor will be able to help you with your overall plan and research questions, a research presentation gives you the best chance of receiving relevant input from academics who may well be involved in the assessment of the piece, so you can gauge what will work and what is less likely to work from their point of view before you begin to write it up. This has the advantage of saving you time, as you will not pursue research avenues that they have convinced you will be of limited use to you, and it will give you a feel for the level of research and presentation required of you within an area of assessment.

There is another, subtler motive for excelling in this task. You might be discussing your work with lecturers and researchers who you may only meet on this occasion, so this is your chance to showcase your talents as a researcher and prove the validity and importance of your research. If you need help later in your course, you will be able to turn to these academics with confidence, knowing that they understand and are impressed by your work. If you choose to pursue your academic career beyond your current course, you will be able to approach your research panel for references, advice and up-to-date information about what is on offer.

Timing

Two approaches tend *not* to work for postgraduates faced with research presentations. They either get in a panic and spend far too long worrying about the event, wondering what it will be like and working on each minute detail of the presentation, to the detriment of their other work, or they rush into the presentation, ill prepared and flustered. The way to avoid these problems is to decide how long you will spend preparing and stick to it, however anxious you become.

The second aspect of the timing of research presentations is their frequency. This will differ from course to course, but you might be in a position to alter their frequency. If, despite all your efforts, you find them a trial and do not find them helpful (and this is unlikely), you can ask that their frequency be reduced. If, as is more probable, you find them useful and enjoyable, you may be able to arrange more frequent meetings, as suggested in Chapter 8.

Managing the task

- *understand what will be involved*: before you work towards a detailed research presentation, ask a series of questions so that you do not have to worry about the practical details. How long will the session last? How long should you spend presenting and how long asking questions of the panel? Where will it be held? How many people will be on the panel listening to the presentation? How wide should your presentation be? Will you be expected to provide a handout of your key presentation points? Will your fellow postgraduates be present? Will you be expected to demonstrate some of your experimental work or simply report upon it?
- *do not panic about your presentation skills*: unlike seminar presentations, in which you might be marked on your presentation performance,

research presentations will not be assessed, so there is no need to spend hours rehearsing how you will present. It is a good idea to run through your presentation aloud before the event, but only so that you can check it will not take too long. The great advantage to you of these unassessed presentations is that you will not be distracted by the presentation techniques you are trying to develop elsewhere. If you have followed the advice offered earlier in this book, you will no longer be terrified about giving a presentation, but even if you are still struggling with some aspects of presentations, you need not worry here: this event is for your benefit, not a test of your presentation expertise. If you have prepared well but know that you will still be nervous and rather tongue-tied, make sure that you have some written material to give out, perhaps in advance, and keep your presentation brief: once a discussion begins, you will relax.

- *be prepared*: the first, and most practical, reason to be prepared is to decide whether you can actually go ahead with a research presentation at the time suggested. If your research relies upon experimental work, you may have to delay a presentation until you have had time to produce and collate results. If you are working on a resource archive that is some distance from your university, and have booked access to the resources there for several weeks, it may not be convenient for you to return to university for your presentation at the suggested date. Unlike some other events in your postgraduate course, it is possible for you to negotiate a change in timing, so do not assume that, just because a date has been set, you have to work to that date if you can show good reasons for delaying it. The second reason for being thoroughly prepared is that you will want to receive comprehensive feedback from the panel. If you are used to giving seminar presentations with relatively little preparation, knowing that you are a naturally good presenter and have a firm grasp of your subject, you might get away with it. For research presentations, you will need to prepare well because you are not being marked on your performance; instead you will be expected to answer a series of questions on your research and discuss in an informed way the many aspects of your work. This inevitably makes the process less predictable and you must be ready for this: preparation is the only guaranteed way to succeed.

- *spend as much time on your questions as on your presentation*: you are not going to be asked to present the final word in any area of research. This is an opportunity to suggest working hypotheses and gauge the reaction to them, glean valuable guidance as to your next research move and gather information about research resources and methodologies. You will not be expected to cover up the shortcomings of your research ideas or mask your anxieties about one particular research path. Instead, you will bring these issues to the attention of the research panel, asking for their help and responding to their suggestions. You have a limited amount of time to do this, so keep asking your questions until time runs out.

- *keep your supervisor informed*: as already suggested, you should not spend so long preparing for a research presentation that it distorts the rest of your personalised timetable, nor will you want to take up too much valuable supervision time teasing out the issues that might be raised at the presentation, as this will simply pre-empt and duplicate the advice that you might receive. However, your supervisor will feel most uncomfortable if you produce ideas, research paths and draft plans for your work at the presentation that you have not revealed before. This will leave you in the position of giving a research presentation to a panel of experts and a startled looking supervisor. To avoid your supervisor being in such a disadvantageous position, make sure that you have submitted at least an outline of your presentation in advance, so that you can work together as a team on the day.

- *revise your plans after the event*: postgraduates can feel that the best possible result from a research presentation is to leave it feeling that the panel have confirmed everything that they thought, fully endorsed their research plans and made no suggestions that will require them to rearrange their personalised timetables. However, this would reduce the value of the presentation to your future work. What you should actively be seeking at a research presentation is input that will both support and challenge your research, opening up a whole new series of research paths. After the presentation, work through what has been said: add to your reading notebooks, revise your research notebook and assess the impact of the suggestions upon your individual research sheets. This may take time but it will be worth it.

- *keep in touch*: make sure that you know who the members of the research panel will be: are they all members of your department? Are there any outside academics who are taking an interest in your work? Will they be regular members of the panel as your course progresses? It is easy enough to get hold of the email addresses of the members of the panel and a brief email thanking them for their advice will lay the groundwork for any future help that you might need. If a member of the panel mentions a theory that is entirely unfamiliar to you or suggests an experimental technique that you have never tried, you might naturally shy away from discussing this in detail on the day, but you need to steel yourself to email the panel member afterwards and ask for more details, perhaps arranging a meeting to discuss the theory or technique in more depth.

- *keep calm*: you might feel awkward if you are asked a question to which you have no answer or blush if you are struggling to express an idea: this will not matter in the slightest. If you have prepared thoroughly, you will be able to continue without difficulty and the research panel will be too interested in your ideas to worry about minor glitches. A greater problem might arise if you have changed your mind about a research idea or radically altered the direction of your research plan, particularly if it was a member of the panel who first suggested it to you. Avoid the temptation to gloss over the issue: be clear about why you have changed your mind and positive about where you are intending to go next. You will have discussed the changes in advance with your supervisor, so you will have support for the points you are making and, again, you will find that the panel are more interested in where you are going than in where you might have been.

▶ Seminar presentations

What is involved?

Seminar presentations must be considered in the overall management of your course. They differ from research presentations in key ways and these will affect how you prepare for them. Unlike less formal seminar papers, presentations might be viewed by a wider audience than your seminar group, so make sure that you find out in advance if this is the case. You might also be expected to produce visual material of a higher quality than in research presentations, so it is worth checking what will be expected of you. They are likely to be held at the same time and in the same room as your usual seminars and this will help you to feel less tense, but you must remind yourself as you prepare that your presentation skills are likely to be assessed and this is a more structured event than your regular seminars, one you will be expected to control, both in terms of timing and content.

Why give them?

As with research presentations, you will have no choice but to give seminar presentations if they form part of your course, but your objectives will differ between the two events. A research presentation is designed to allow you to ask questions and outline theories, sharing tentative research ideas with the panel and asking for their help. A seminar presentation is intended to allow you to demonstrate your grasp of an area of your subject. You will still not be asked to provide a definitive answer to all the questions your work has raised, but you will be expected to produce a coherent pattern of thought that stands alone and sustain an argument for the length of the presentation.

To some extent, seminar presentations take you beyond your current course. If you present well and are able to articulate your ideas and argue your case convincingly, you will be moving towards a professional standpoint that might be essential to your future career. Within seminar presentations you are aiming to produce a polished performance, concerned to listen to the suggestions your audience makes, but essentially presenting a viewpoint you can support in the face of questions and discussion. It is not unheard of for course sponsors and potential employers to view these presentations, so be aware of the possible long-term benefits of giving a convincing performance.

Timing

This may be dictated by your term's set timetable, but you will be given enough time to prepare adequately. The time you allow for your preparation will depend upon two factors. Firstly, a group presentation will require more preparation time than an individual presentation, as you will have to arrange for group rehearsals to dovetail your individual contributions. It is clear that you will have to include this preparation time within your personalised timetable so you are not forced into last-minute preparations. The second factor to consider is the percentage of marks allocated to the presentational aspects of the event and the percentage given over to the content. This may not affect your overall preparation time but will have an impact upon the way in which you spend that time.

Managing the task

- *ask questions*: as with research presentations, make sure that you know exactly what will be expected of you. How long will the presentation last? Will there be a question and answer session afterwards or should your presentation be designed to stimulate a more general discussion? What equipment will be available; what visual aids will you be expected to produce? Will other seminar groups be watching you?
- *study other presentations*: as you watch the presentations given by other members of your seminar group, you will, of course, be interested in what is being said, but you should also be considering the presentation techniques they are using, the ways in which they support their arguments with visual aids and the methods they employ to encourage and then control the discussion that arises from the presentation. You will not necessarily want to employ all their methods but you will at least want to consider using them.
- *seek the help you need*: there should be help available if you find presentations difficult. Presentation workshops might be the best starting point, but remember that your fellow students will also be able to help. If you form a rehearsal group, you can meet regularly, taking it in turns to present and sharing advice as you all develop your presentation skills.

If you find that you work well together, make the effort to keep the group together, meeting whenever any of you have to face a presentation.

- *find other events at which to practise*: one of the easiest ways to perfect your presentation skills is to grasp every opportunity to practise. Speaking up at a seminar, contributing to a discussion group, leading undergraduate seminars, presenting to meetings at work: all these will help. If your opportunities are limited, consider becoming involved in a student group that will give you the chance to contribute to meetings or lead discussions. This need not be the debating society, if that seems too daunting, any student group can give you the chance to speak to an audience.

- *plan thoroughly*: although you will obviously want to plan the content, make sure that you also plan the logistics of giving a presentation. When will you give out your handouts? How long will it take to produce the visual aids such as overhead projector acetates or data projector slides? Will you have to do further research especially for this event and how will this affect your personalised timetable? Do you have time to attend presentation workshops? If the presentation is a group effort, when can you all meet to discuss the content and rehearse the presentation?

- *check with your supervisor that your argument is credible*: you will not be able to devote too much supervision time to a seminar presentation, but you could show your plan to your supervisor, perhaps by email, just to make sure that you have not overlooked any gaping holes in your argument or made any assumptions that are likely to trip you up.

- *produce more material than you think you will use*: if there is to be a question and answer session once you have finished speaking, you will be aware of the general direction the questions are likely to follow, so prepare additional material (perhaps in the form of an extra handout) to which you can refer as you face the questions. You might also want to ask a fellow student to prepare a question in advance for which you have an impressive answer, so that if the silence at the end of your presentation extends to unbearable proportions, your colleague can be ready to get things started by asking the question. It is unlikely that you will need this question, so make sure that your colleague only asks it as a last resort, but it will reduce your stress if you know that it is there as a failsafe option.

- *your presentation is part of a continuing process*: in your relief at having achieved a successful presentation, try to remember that you will need to make a note of what went well and how you might improve your technique next time. This is particularly important if you have identified presentations as one of the areas you would like to work on for your skills inventory. You will forget the details of the event remarkably quickly, so make notes on your performance as soon as you can. No single presentation is going to make or break your course, so see each one as an opportunity to improve.

- *using the feedback*: it can be difficult to take in what is being said to you in the minutes after a presentation. You are so relieved it is over that you simply smile vacantly and long to sit down again. Despite this natural response, make notes of what is said, both about your presentation technique and the contents of the presentation, and go back over these notes later, updating your reading and research notebooks, your skills inventory and your research sheets.

▶ Conference papers

What is involved?

The style of delivering conference papers varies widely between disciplines, from the simple reading of a paper to sleek performances more akin to commerical presentations. In all cases some general rules will apply. You will have a set time to give your paper, with further time set aside for questions and answers. You will have submitted a proposal for your paper so the organisers of the conference, and the audience, will know what to expect and will be ready to ask relevant questions. You will be introduced by a conference organiser and this is one of the pleasures of giving a conference paper: from being nervous and tentative about what you are doing, you can be transformed into a far more confident speaker during the minute or so it takes to introduce you, when the organiser will extol your virtues as an academic and explain what you will be trying to do during your paper. A paper can be a finished piece of work, perhaps a chapter from your thesis or dissertation, or a résumé of work in progress, in which case this will be made clear to the audience, who will tailor their questions and suggestions accordingly.

Why give them?

You are most unlikely to be required to give a conference paper as part of your course, but there are three compelling reasons why you might want to do so. Firstly, it is an excellent opportunity to share your work with a wide-ranging audience of academics and gain their feedback. Secondly, it gives you the chance to network, as members of the audience will remember your paper for some time and will be happy to support your work in the future. Thirdly, if you intend to continue beyond your current course or pursue an academic career, your CV will be vastly improved by the addition of a conference paper you have given. There might be a further reason to give a paper: conferences proceedings are sometimes lodged on the Internet, and occasionally conference organisers are able to arrange for the papers to be published in a journal or collated to produce a book, and this might encourage you to give a paper.

Timing

This is crucial. It takes time to prepare a paper, more time than you might expect, and this can interrupt your personalised timetable. If you are delivering a paper based upon a section of your extended research project or an article you have already written, it might take less time but you will still have to tailor your paper to the conference theme. Before producing your proposal, think carefully about how much time you will have to devote to the task. If you cannot fit it into your timetable at this stage, remember that there will be other opportunities later in your course.

Managing the task

- *prepare*: before you begin to prepare, indeed, before you submit your proposal, think about how you might reuse material you have already produced; a draft chapter of your thesis or dissertation might be ideal for the purpose. This is the time to go back to research sheets that you have discarded to see if you could rework any of your earlier ideas. A seminar presentation can be a good opening point for a more extended conference paper, as can an essay that you felt was restricted by the word count. The general rule here is never to abandon any research that might be useful to you in the future and reuse work that can be adapted for a new set of circumstances.

- *be clear about the conference structure*: avoid being caught out by the practical details of your contribution to a conference. If you are speaking after lunch, for example, you might need to produce some visual aids to help the audience to concentrate. If you are given a single speaker slot, you will be holding the audience for perhaps 40–50 minutes, giving your paper and answering questions. If you are given a multiple speaker slot, you might deliver your paper, then listen to another paper before jointly fielding audience questions. You might be asked to prepare a synopsis of your paper several weeks before the event and this must be scheduled into your timetable.

- *footnotes*: you will not be producing a paper for a conference in the same way as you write an essay, in that you will make notes to yourself on your paper, perhaps reminding you to slow down, or highlighting sections where you might be happy to leave the written page to talk less formally to the audience. You might also have a series of backup documents, showing details of experiments you have not included in detail in the paper, or copies of texts and images that you have as visual aids, but for which you also need your own notes. Regardless of these differences, it is still important that you footnote your paper. You will recognise the value of this as soon as you are asked a tricky question: in your excitement, or nervousness, you might forget the date of a publication, but a glance at your footnotes will save you from embarrassment. Footnotes will also be necessary if you publish your paper; the excitement of being told that a publication will arise from the conference can quickly turn to frustration if you then have to spend days going back over your paper to create a set of footnotes.

- *spoken and written language*: when you have prepared your paper and begin to practise it, remember that spoken and written language are subtly, but fundamentally, different. If you do no more than read a paper as you wrote it, you will sounded stilted and distance yourself from your audience. To avoid this, make sure that during your first read through of the paper you mark those phrases that sound odd to you when spoken aloud, then revise the paper to soften them. If you rehearse enough (and this will mean rehearsing the paper at least six or seven times), revising the text each time, you will be familiar enough with the material to allow your language to be more relaxed on the day and move from written to spoken language. Of course, if your conference paper is to take the form of a presentation, you will be preparing as if for a seminar presentation, working most probably from a series of prompt cards rather than a fully developed script.

- *attend several conferences*: you will not want to be undermined in giving your paper by the unfamiliarity of the conference format. Academic conferences are quite different from other academic events and it is a good idea to have attended several of them before you give a paper, so that you become accustomed to the atmosphere of conferences and the ways in which they are run.

- *meet the audience*: a sea of unfamiliar faces can be overwhelming when you are about to give your paper, so make sure that you talk to a few members of the audience before it is time for you to speak. You will be tempted to stand to one side, running through your paper in your mind, but you will know it well enough by now, however nervous you feel, so instead force yourself to socialise: you will be grateful for the smiling faces of the people you have just met when you face the audience from the stage and you will have undertaken some useful networking.

- *relaxation techniques*: nerves will always be a useful asset as you face giving a paper. They will ensure that you perform well, but you must prevent them from undermining you. The good news is that, if you can force your body to relax, you can fool it into believing that the situation is not quite so terrifying. There are four easy relaxation techniques you can employ to keep your nerves under control so that you can use them to sharpen your performance. Firstly, notice what your fingers and toes are doing. If they are clenched, and they probably will be, make a conscious effort to open your fingers wide and relax your toes by wiggling them. Next, think about your tongue. By now it is probably stuck to the roof of your rather dry mouth. If you relax your tongue, you will be able to relax your whole upper body, allowing you to breathe more deeply. Once your tongue is relaxed, you can work on your neck and shoulders. If you can drop your shoulders this will help; if you are one of those people who find this difficult, imagine a thread attached to the back of your head and think of it being drawn upwards. This will force you to lower your chin and raise your head, which will have the automatic effect of dropping your shoulders. Finally, control your breathing. If you just try to take deep breaths when you are nervous, you might risk making yourself dizzy, so instead breath out completely and then close your mouth. Keep your mouth closed until you feel a real need to breathe, but then rather than consciously breathing in, simply open your mouth. Your diaphragm will draw air into your lungs without any effort on your part and you will feel more relaxed. This can take some practice, but if you place your hand over your diaphragm (between your chest and your stomach) as you do this, you will eventually feel your diaphragm spring outwards as you open your mouth, and this can be very reassuring when you are sitting on a platform preparing to give a paper. Nobody will notice you are doing it, but you will feel better and far more ready to stand up and speak.

- *enjoy yourself*: it might sound like a tall order to suggest that you should enjoy yourself whilst you give a paper, but it is possible, even during your first paper, to begin to enjoy the response of the audience, to be caught up in what you want to say and become engaged in the discussion that follows. If you have this as one of your aims, however unlikely it seems, you will be pleased to find that it can be, indeed it should be, a pleasure to give a conference paper.

▶ Publication

What is involved?

There are various ways in which you might publish your writing during your postgraduate course and several reasons why you might want to do this. If you would like to extend your writing skills or try out new areas of writing, you could contribute to newsletters, research bulletins or your student or university newspaper. If, on the other hand, your intention is to publish your academic work, you will probably be working towards writing an article for a journal or periodical or producing material for inclusion on an Internet site. You might also be thinking about your thesis in terms of a book publication. Publication is an exciting aspect of your postgraduate course: the chance to publish your work can help to keep you motivated.

Why become published?

As with conference papers, your answer to this will depend to some extent upon your ambitions. If you hope to pursue an academic career, publication might be crucial to your success. If you intend to apply for a further course, a publication will enhance your application. However, even if you do not have plans to advance your academic life beyond your current course, it is satisfying to have some of your work published, to know that your research will be read and enjoyed beyond your university.

Timing

Always consider publication as early as you possibly can. Lead times for publication, the time that it takes to transform your initial proposal into a printed article, can be extensive: up to two years is not unusual. Clearly, if you would like to be published in time to highlight your achievement to prospective course convenors or employers, you will need to act quickly. You will not want to submit an unpolished article, full of undeveloped ideas, but equally if you leave it too long it may be too late, so push yourself to think about this option as soon as you have produced an extended piece of work, perhaps for a lengthy seminar presentation or a conference paper. If you intend to contribute to an Internet site, the lead time should be far shorter, but you will still need to work up your ideas into a relevant article, and there might be a list of articles waiting for inclusion on the site.

Managing the task

- *be aware of copyright*: there is not the space within this book to explore all aspects of copyright law, but you are already conversant with the problems of plagiarism, and now you need to protect your own work. The simplest way to tackle this complex issue is simply to ask about copyright when you are offered the chance to publish, especially if you are contributing to an Internet site.
- *know your journals*: because it is time consuming to prepare work for publication, it is tempting to produce an article and simply submit it to

a series of journals simultaneously, in the hope that it might be picked up and selected for publication. Apart from the obvious problem of multiple offers of publication, this random approach tends to be unproductive. Each journal has its own bias in terms of the type of article in which it is interested; this might be a historical bias, an editorial angle or a preference for highly theoretical articles or largely descriptive articles and so on. It is more effective to target your articles in a very focused way. Decide upon the specific area of your research on which you would like to write, study the relevant journals carefully and make sure that your finished article fits the general profile of articles within the journal. There is no need to stray from what you believe or gloss over your research findings, but you will be approaching a journal with an awareness that your article will sit happily in one of its future issues.

- *reusing your material*: although submitting the same article to several journals simultaneously can cause problems, there is no reason why you should not adapt your material and produce two or three articles, written from different angles, from one area of your research. If you have given a conference paper, you can adapt the material for publication, knowing that it has already received a positive response.

- *know exactly what is required*: journals differ in their submission requirements and they may simply reject your article if you do not adhere to their format, so avoid such an elementary problem by finding out exactly how long your article should be and the form in which it should be presented.

- *gather plenty of material*: within an essay or piece of coursework, you have a clearly defined frame of reference and so will limit your research to cover your immediate needs. Within a dissertation or thesis, you can use up most of your research; if you occasionally make a point that is only flimsily supported by your evidence, you can leave the research question open for the reader to consider before moving on to your more substantiated sections of writing. Within an article, you will be trying to present a clear argument in favour of the point you are making, backed up by ample evidence, and this can use up more material than you would expect. When you include the preparation of an article within your personalised timetable, give yourself a little extra time for your research. In this way you can ensure that you have some extra material, evidence that you may not use but that is ready if you feel that your argument is inadequately supported at any point.

- *be determined*: the figures speak for themselves. You only have to visualise the number of academics who must be submitting articles for publication each year to realise that the competition is fierce. If you wait for a response from one journal before you get on with writing your next article, you will have completed your course before you have tried all those journals you think might publish your work. Once you have submitted an article, move on to the next one and try to relax about what is happening to the first. You need to manage your timetable so that you do not spend too much time writing articles because there is so much else to do, but do not sit back and wait for a result before you move on to the next opportunity.

- *it might take time*: if publication is important to you, you will have to be dogged about your pursuit of this goal. Whilst you are writing an article, look around for other opportunities, such as conferences from which papers might be published, books that will require contributions or home-produced university research booklets or magazines. You do not have the time to concentrate upon this aspect of your postgraduate experience to the exclusion of more immediate tasks, but you could usefully set aside some time in your personalised timetable just to contemplate the possibilities open to you, discuss publication with your supervisor and consider how you might adapt your work to meet a wider audience.

The challenges of presentations and publication can be great, but so too can the rewards. Conferences will open your eyes to the wider world of academia, whilst publication offers you the chance to reach a new audience. However, all these activities, important as they will become in your course, are going to be just part of the process of working towards your ultimate goal: that of producing an extensive piece of independent research, a thesis or dissertation, and it is on this area we will focus in the next chapter.

Spot guide

Key points to remember from this chapter:

- research presentations are designed to help you, so use them for your benefit
- always be sure about whether your presentation skills are being assessed
- make extensive notes after research presentations
- network at research presentations and conferences
- timing will always be crucial: plan for success
- prepare at least as thoroughly for a research presentation as for a seminar presentation
- confirm all the practical details of each presentation well in advance
- master your nerves and then use them to your advantage
- prepare for the questions you might be asked after a presentation
- include preparation time for conference papers in your personalised timetable
- consider all publication options: conference papers, the Internet, book contributions and journal articles
- remain aware of the long-term advantages of presenting and publishing
- take an overview of what you can reasonably achieve in the time available to you and how you might benefit from your efforts

10 Writing up your Research

Troubleshooting guide

Use this chapter for help in the following areas:

- if you are daunted by the word count for your dissertation, research report or thesis
- if you are worried about how to write up your research in the time available
- if you are not sure whether you think through a problem best by writing about it
- if you get bored when you write extensively
- if you are concerned about how to produce a final plan for your written work
- if you are unclear about how to develop research sheets into realistic plans
- if you would like to know how a final plan should look
- if you tend to work at the last minute and are concerned by this
- if you need more information on spider charts, flow charts or brainstorming
- if you tend to produce work that is over or under the stipulated word count
- if you hate rewriting your work
- if you are uncertain about how to make the best use of drafts and rewrites
- if you are anxious about how to create a bibliography
- if your writing style is worrying you

The thought of writing up an independent research project can put you off the idea of undertaking a postgraduate course altogether. Until you produce a thesis or dissertation, or a series of extensive reports on experimental work, you cannot be sure that you can achieve this goal. It is inevitable that you will have the occasional panic, that sometimes things will go less smoothly than you would like, but you will be guided through the process. If you have been concerned about the prospect of writing up your research, you may be surprised to find that, in the earlier part of your course, you think about the task very little. Although you will always be aware of this as a goal, in the first stages of your course your time will be taken up with other considerations. In a taught course you will have lectures and seminars to attend, assessed pieces of work to produce and, perhaps, presentations to give. It is only later that your research will become pressing. Even if you are undertaking a research-based course, you may undertake months of research before you begin to write it up. This is a good thing: you need time to develop your ideas and test your hypotheses before you commit yourself to writing up your work. You also need some practice in producing academic work and you might decide that you need to turn to a study guide that deals solely with this issue. However, you can save yourself a lot of anguish if you take control of some key aspects of writing up your research as early as possible, and it is on these that this chapter will focus.

▶ Timing

The way in which you approach your writing up will vary according to the course you are taking, the work you are producing and your preferred methods of working. You might spend eight months studying your subject and devote only the last two months of your course to writing up your research. If you are undertaking a vocational, work-based study, your initial results might be available for writing up within a few weeks. You might work well under pressure, writing up only as a deadline approaches, or you might prefer to produce sections as you progress, happy to revise your work as the situation develops. If you are taking a three-year doctoral course, you may write your first draft chapter within a couple of months or you might write nothing that could truly be called part of your thesis until year three. Whatever your circumstances, you can ensure that the timing is working for you rather than against you:

- *your timing is unique to you*: you will, no doubt, discuss your plans for writing up your research with your fellow postgraduates, but remember that your timing has to be unique to your circumstances, so do not become overly anxious because some of your colleagues appear to be ahead of you. If you are earning money during much of your course, you might have to plan for a last-minute push to get everything written up, but you should not overlook the fact that you might simply be the sort of person who likes the challenge of a final dash to the end, would be bored by months of draft sections or chapters and will perform best if left to work in this way. If you prefer to write up early, you will be reassured by the feeling that you have the task under control from the earliest stages, but remember that you will have to rewrite some sections as your research progresses, so you will need to keep an open mind about what you have already produced.

- *discuss timing with your supervisor*: your supervisor is in the best position to advise you as to timing, so make sure that this is one of the issues you tackle early on. Supervisors sometimes have a tendency to assume that you know how the system works, will be relaxed about the process of writing up and will have the timing under control. If this is not the case, make it clear that you will need some help and, as importantly, some reassurance as your work progresses. As with other issues, this is best done once you have put in the groundwork. A casual mention of writing up on your part will probably produce a vague answer, but if you produce your research sheets and plans, ready to talk about how you intend to conquer the research and when you will begin your writing up, your supervisor will be able to discuss the situation with you in a more detailed and helpful way.

- *how do you think best?* this is going to be a crucial factor in how you approach writing up your research. Some postgraduates find they need to write things down in order to put their thoughts in order. These pieces of writing need not be entire chapters, or even sections, they might be synopses of your research to date. Other postgraduates find that the very act of writing solidifies their thoughts too much and hinders the free thinking for which they are aiming. You are unlikely to have given this much thought before, so take time early on to consider which method works best for you and try to plan your tasks accordingly. There is one other factor to take into account: how long is your course? If you are studying over several years, it can be difficult to recall all the nuances and inferences of your early research when you return to it after a year or so, and in this case some level of writing up, however sketchy, makes sense and will save you valuable time in the end. If you find writing a potentially stifling process, you can ensure that this informal writing up does not prevent you from making connections: a brief overview of your findings, followed by a series of bullet point suggestions as to how this piece of research might fit into your overall plan will suffice.

- *vary your tasks*: extensive writing involves different mental processes from researching, reading or producing a short essay or presentation. During your research you will be keeping an open mind, searching for connections and remaining open to suggestions and new research paths that might emerge. Writing a short essay, report or preparing for a presentation will not take up all your intellectual energy: you will still be thinking about your dissertation, thesis or next piece of assessed work, dovetailing the various activities that you have been set. By the time you come to write up your final piece, you will have a firm plan in place and will be focused on this one task, concerned to demonstrate that your hypothesis is supportable, you have covered all the relevant research areas and you can make a persuasive argument for your viewpoint. At times you will feel as if you are taming your material: there will be so much to say and suddenly there are too few words with which to say it, you are aware of competing demands and are marshalling your evidence to support one argument in the face of others. At other times you will feel that you have too little evidence, the facts are just out of your reach and your argument, whilst valid, is in need of more support. You can even out the process in the first stages of your writing up by varying your tasks, spending most of your time writing up your research, but also checking your reading notebooks (this will remind you of any texts to which you need to refer), refreshing your research notebook (have you included every piece of research in your plan?) and perfecting your plan: you will have a plan in place, but is it as detailed as you now need it to be? Will it support your efforts throughout the whole of the writing up process?

- *leave yourself plenty of time*: when you are preparing to write up your research, you will have a plan in place and will have decided how long it should take you to write, but you may have forgotten some key tasks, such as the time it will take to produce graphs and charts, obtain photographs or the time you will need for supervisions as the writing up progresses. You will be checking your work, but will need to leave time for others to check it as well, remembering that they might not be as efficient as you, and you will also need to leave a reasonable amount of time for it to be professionally bound, if you are required to do this. Make sure that you have warned people in advance if you would like them to check your work and found out how long they would like you to leave for this. Confirm the waiting times for your university bindery: they can be worryingly long at those times of the year when dissertations and theses are due for submission.

- *be positive*: most successful postgraduates could tell you stories of nights with no sleep and days full of anxiety as they wrote up their research, not to mention the frenzied work of the last few days or weeks as they checked their work and submitted it for binding. All these accounts might be true and some would argue that this level of panic is a necessary part of the postgraduate experience, but you can reduce your anxiety levels by refusing to become negative about the process. It is by no means unusual for postgraduates to have no clear idea of the title of their dissertations as they begin a course, nor is it anything to be concerned about if your thesis title changes several times as your work develops: you are not expected to be an expert in your field and know the outcome of your research before you have had the chance to carry out the work. At all times, remember that you will produce your research project on time, it will reflect the work you have put into it and you will be pleased with the result.

▶ Planning

Planning your dissertation, thesis or extended research report is the single most important task in successfully managing this aspect of your course. It will also be different from any other planning you have undertaken in the past in several key ways. It will take longer than you might expect, often longer than the writing up itself takes, as you might be planning it, in some form or another, for most of your course. You will probably have to alter your plan, perhaps radically, as your research progresses. You will also have to remain open to the possibility of employing several planning methods in order to tease out the issues raised by your research and then present them in the most persuasive and appropriate way. Even if planning is not your strongest skill, you can take control of the process:

- *be prepared to change your mind*: it can be enormously frustrating to have a plan in place, convinced that it will work, and then be forced to change your mind, either because your research throws up unexpected results or your supervisor suggests a new way of working. Chapter 5 dealt with this area in some detail, but the key point to remember here is that if you find yourself writing up your research from the sixth or seventh version of your plan, this is not because you have been woolly-minded, it is because you have thrashed out all the issues raised by your research, remained responsive to the direction that it has taken and are now writing up from the best possible plan.
- *use your research sheets and plans*: you will have been creating research sheets and several of these will have been developed into full-scale plans for individual pieces of work such as essays, papers or presentations. You will also have been developing a research sheet for your final piece, incorporating research references as your course progresses, but it would be a mistake to write directly from this research sheet. Instead, you will need to adapt this sheet into a workable plan and this is done by

reassessing each point on the sheet and checking back to every other sheet and draft plan you have produced in order to assess its relevance to the work you are about to undertake. You will not produce a full, draft plan until shortly before you begin to write up and this will then be discussed with your colleagues and supervisor. Even at this stage, you will have identified some areas that need a little more research before you are ready to commit yourself to paper, but this is normal and will allow you to vary your tasks a little as you write up.

* *plan everything*: the ideal situation is to write up from a plan that leaves you very little room for error and allows you to focus on the writing without the distraction of too many unfinished tasks or concerns about how long each section will take to write and how many words it will use. The plan outlined at the end of this section will give you an idea of how it might look.

* *planning methods*: you are unlikely to use one single planning method in the creation of your final plan and it is useful to assess the methods available before you begin to make the plan, as different sections of it will respond well to particular methods. However, the most important point to remember about planning methods is that you need to know which methods work best for you, regardless of the tasks ahead of you. A planning method that works well for one person can simply confuse another, so think back to a situation when you have had to plan under pressure, perhaps in examinations or preparing a plan for an earlier piece of work, and decide what suits you best. Although new ways of planning appear all the time in study skills guides, there are several principal methods that you might choose to try for different aspects of your plan. I will take, for the purposes of these examples, a dissertation section considering the achievements and failures of a modern UK prime minister.

Spider diagrams

These are useful if you are trying to think widely around an area of your research whilst remaining focused on your main objective. You write key words in a central circle (the 'body' of your spider), and then build up a plan around this circle by adding more circles as you think of ideas (creating the 'legs' of the spider). As you can see from Figure 10.1, planning in this way will allow you to think around the subject without ever losing sight of your goal and is therefore useful if you are concerned you might be led astray from your main research path. Once you have created the spider, you will automatically have your main sections and subsections in place (note how the education section has been divided into subsections and further divided into sub-subsections, making another, smaller 'spider') and you can make connections between the various 'legs' of the spider.

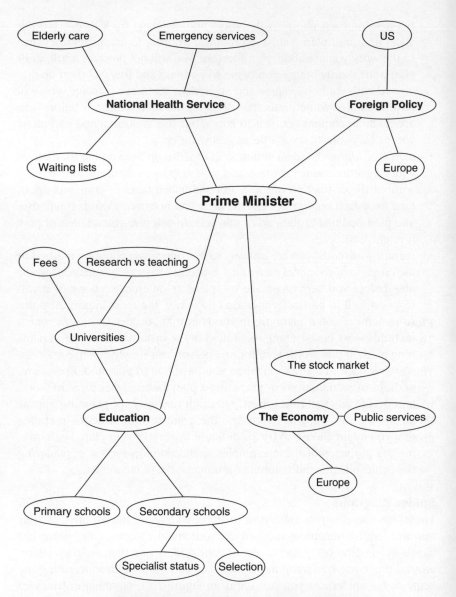

Figure 10.1 Example of a spider diagram

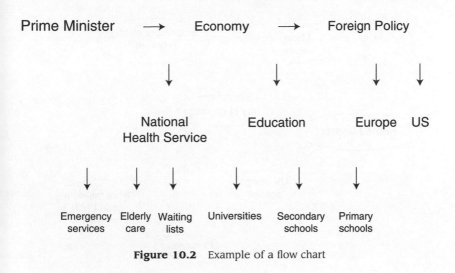

Figure 10.2 Example of a flow chart

Flow charts

These are helpful if you have a mass of data to control and bring into a plan. They will give your plan a logical development, as Figure 10.2 demonstrates. The potential disadvantage of flow charts in planning is that they can become restrictive as you try to chart a perfectly logical flow. You might feel forced to decide upon the order of your points at the earliest stages of planning and it can be disconcerting if you have to place new, unexpected boxes into the chart.

Brainstorming

This is a popular method of planning, particularly if you feel that you are reaching a dead end in your planning or are having trouble getting out of a rut. You take a large piece of paper, write your key phrase in the centre and add your thoughts randomly to the plan (Figure 10.3). In this type of plan no one idea is foregrounded over another in the early stages. You will end up with a messy piece of paper, with all sorts of ideas jotted down. This is especially effective if you can persuade a few friends to join you; they will be happy to add their contributions precisely because it is so messy: nobody need feel responsible for where an idea might end up in your final plan and each person is persuaded to have a go. The danger with this method of planning is that it can confuse you, so it should be used only when you really do need to think as widely as possible and in a creative way. You must take charge of the process once the brainstorming is complete, determinedly

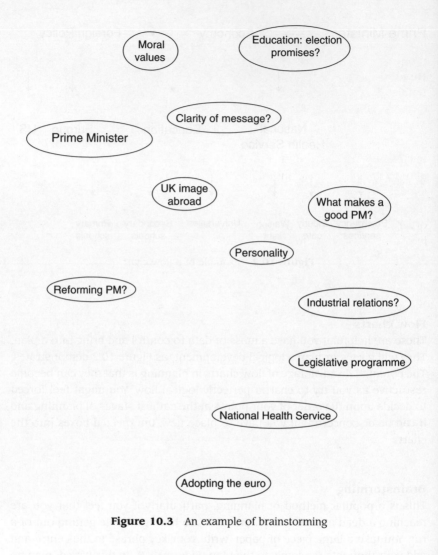

Figure 10.3 An example of brainstorming

disregarding those ideas that will not help you and placing the useful ideas into an ordered structure.

Headings

Both spider charts and brainstorming sheets tend to be rearranged into plans divided into headings, as this is the easiest plan to read and understand at a glance once you are engaged in writing up your research, but you might decide that you work best by using headings for your initial planning, simply making a list of headings and then arranging them into subheadings as your plan progresses. This method of planning tends to work best if you are clear about your objectives and happy to plunge into a full-scale plan. It gives you the option of including topics you might later discard and gives a sense of order to your thoughts. The potential disadvantage is that you may be locked into a finalised plan before you have given yourself the chance to think around your subject widely enough. Your headings, subheadings and sub-subheadings might look like this:

Prime Minister

Economy   Stock market
Fear of recession
Interest rates
Foreign investment

National Health Service   Waiting lists
NHS structure
Elderly care
Emergency services

Education   Universities   Fees
Admission policies
Student numbers
Secondary schools   League tables
Subject options
Vocational courses
Primary schools   Parental choice
Performance targets
Preschool provision?

It is clear that a variety of planning methods can be employed as you make your plan and each has advantages and disadvantages. If you vary your approach, using different methods for separate sections, you will have the best chance of creating a comprehensive and relevant plan, but remain aware that some methods will not suit your ways of working and abandon them as soon as you feel they are hindering rather than helping your progress. Whichever methods you use, you will be aiming to produce a plan that is comprehensive enough to leave you with no nasty surprises yet flexible enough to allow you to develop your work as you write. With the example used here, where the analysis of the prime minister's performance is just one section of a dissertation and is intended to take up no more than 6,000 words, the detailed plan might look like this:

Prime minister
Note for beginning: link back to last section – need full introductory section? Remember to frame within historical overview.

Economy	Stock market	*include decade statistics*
3,000 words	Fear of recession	*link to US experience – Devoir, Mills,*
(by week six)		*Long's thesis*
	Interest rates	*include most recent figures*
	Foreign investment	*need more data?*

National Health Service	Waiting lists	*refer to Wilson and Smith*
1,200 words		*article?*
(by week nine)	NHS structure	*get government graph –*
		copyright?
	Elderly care	*relevant?*
	Emergency care	*too large an area to include?*

Education	Universities	Fees	*media review*
1,200 words		Admission policies	*Taylor and*
(by week three			*Crowe*
of vacation)		Student numbers	*interviews*
			here?
	Secondary schools	League tables	*Cullock,*
			Knight
		Subject options	*compare with*
			Europe?
		Vocational courses	*comparison*
			charts
	Primary schools	Parental choice	*case study*
		Performance targets	*my investigation*
		Preschool provision?	*enough space?*

It is worth noting some of the details included in this plan. A word count has been given for each section: this is crucial. You need to be able to visualise the overall shape of your work, the way in which it will develop and how it will look once it is complete. You can only do this by allocating words to each section you intend to produce; in this way you will be reflecting the relative importance or complexity of each section and the amount of evidence you intend to include. Although the total word count for this section is 6,000 words, the allocated word count here is only 90 per cent of that, 5,400 words, because there are enough variables in the plan to suppose that more words might be needed at the last minute. The timetable for progress has also been sketched in. This will link to your personalised timetable, as you may be writing up your research whilst you continue with lectures and seminars and so you will need to incorporate the writing up process within your overall scheme of work. Both the word count and the timing will, of course, be open to change, but you have a better chance of keeping on track if you include them in an estimated way in your plan. The sources of data have been noted beside each subsection and in this way your notebooks will have become an integral part of your planning. You will still need to take one last look through your reading and research notebooks and the research sheet or sheets on which you based your plan before discussing the plan with your supervisor, just to make sure that you have not missed anything.

This plan is not rigid: it includes some notes where the writer is querying whether the word count will be sufficient to include all the potential material, whether some sections will remain relevant as the work progresses and whether there is enough material to support certain sections. This need not be a cause for anxiety: no plan will be a definitive account of what you are going to write. It should be detailed enough for you to feel secure in what you are doing and it must feel safe. That is, it must include notes of areas where you might need to do more research and also queries to yourself about whether certain arguments should be pursued. In this way, you will feel reassured that you will not forget anything, but you will also feel free to make slight amendments to content, tone and structure as you write.

▶ Word count

As you contemplate a postgraduate course, the thought of producing a dissertation or thesis can be daunting: it can seem like simply too many words to produce, probably far more than you have written before. The word count itself will vary, depending upon your course, and so too will the structure and presentation of your research project, but whatever the restraints and requirements placed upon you, it is far more probable, however unlikely it seems at the outset, that you will find the word count too little for your needs than that you will run out of things to write. There are several aspects of your word count that you must keep in mind:

- *ignore the word count at the outset*: try not to let the earlier part of your course be overshadowed by the thought of all those words. A postgraduate course is designed to develop your skills both as a researcher and a writer, and once you have written a 5,000 word essay or report, a 20,000 word dissertation will seem far easier. Once you have produced a 15,000 word draft chapter for your thesis, you will see that 80,000 or 90,000 words will hardly be enough to contain all the areas that you want to cover.

- *be clear about the word count when you prepare your plan*: it is best not to assume that any word count you have been given is as simple as it looks. Whatever your course prospectus might say, check with your supervisor and the departmental secretaries just how long the word count is this year and how much leeway you might have. You also need to be clear about the details: will your footnotes and bibliography be included in the word count? If you go over the word count, do you have a percentage of the total to play with? If you are under the word count (most unlikely), at what point will you be penalised for this?

- *allocate a word count to every stage of your plan*: this will ensure that you keep the shape of your overall work in your mind and will alert you to potential problems if your word count, once you begin to write, does not match your plan.

- *use the word count to your advantage*: word counts are not handed out arbitrarily. You have been given a word count because it is considered that you can achieve all that is necessary within it, so you can feel confident that your work will eventually fit the word count. You will not have produced a better or more impressive dissertation or thesis simply because you have exceeded the given word count; it is more probable that you have had difficulty in harnessing your material and controlling your argument.

- *let your word count develop naturally*: word counts are peculiar things. If you begin to write focusing principally on what you have to say and how you will say it, you will find that, in most cases, the word count takes care of itself. Your computer will allow you to check your word count easily as you progress, so if you are worried you can check it every few paragraphs, but do not let this become a distraction. Of course, it is heartening to check your word count every now and then, just to remind yourself of how well you are doing, but if it is a little over or marginally under, try to keep going until the end of the section before you become too concerned: word counts have a way of righting themselves as work progresses.

* *analyse the problem if it persists*: if you find that you are seriously astray from your word count at the end of a section, now is the time to examine what is going wrong. If your word count persistently goes wrong, talk to your supervisor rather than worrying about it alone, but there are aspects of your word count you can examine before you bring in expert help. If your word count is too low, this can be rectified at a later stage relatively easily. Perhaps you just tend to write in a very concise style. If you continue with a low word count, you can go back to the sections later and insert more material or adopt a more developed style of writing. If, as is more likely, you are exceeding your planned word count at each stage, in one way this can be a good thing. It is usually easy to revise your work once it is written and make your writing style more concise, and this might be all you need to do in order to bring it back within the word count. If the problem is more about content, consider whether you have more to say than you had expected in this section. This is no problem at all, as long as you can adapt your word count later by reducing sections of your plan. Amend your plan at this stage rather than hoping to reduce your word count haphazardly as you go along: this can lead to greater problems in the future.

More problematically, you could be moving away from the structure you had set up in your plan: are you wandering down research paths that you have only discovered as you write? Have you missed out a section of your plan? Have you included all the sections that you had identified in your plan as only possible inclusions, to be left out if your word count rose too high? Do you find it difficult to exclude evidence not directly relevant to the point you are making? Are you beginning to lose sight of your objective? Are you starting to doubt your hypothesis? Are you losing confidence in what you have to say? Do you find the subject so fascinating that you just cannot stop writing about everything you have ever learnt about it? If you suspect that the answer to any of these questions is 'yes', stop writing. Go back over your work and be ruthless: where are you meandering away from your plan? Having identified the problem area (perhaps with the help of your supervisor), be determined about cutting down your writing or going back to an earlier section and adding to it. Editing down your word count can be surprisingly painful at first, but once you see how much sharper your writing is becoming, and how much more focused your argument is when you make these cuts, you will begin to enjoy the process of reading your work critically and editing it back down to a manageable word count. If you find this process difficult, and worry about the words you are cutting out, remember that it is only by being firm now that you will have the chance to include all the other arguments you want to raise later in the work. If you are concerned about removing material, save your deleted sections as separate documents and review them a week or so later. You will see instantly whether you were right to make the cuts.

▶ Drafts and rewrites

Writing up your research will create reams of paper, some of which contain vital pieces of data, some of which include perfect phrases and well-organised paragraphs and some of which, inevitably, contain writing you will discard as too clumsy, too insubstantial or too naive to include in your final work. Producing work in draft and then rewriting sections of your extended research project can seem at first sight to be a real nuisance, particularly if you have not worked in this way before. Never allow yourself to become concerned about the number of rewrites that your colleagues are undertaking: some students find it easier to compose their thoughts and marshal their arguments by writing them out, others prefer to do most of the work in the planning stages, rewriting only when it becomes absolutely necessary and keeping draft work to a minimum. The best way to approach this aspect of your writing up is to see it as a positive part of the process of producing the best possible dissertation, extended report or thesis, and there are positive steps that you can take to achieve this:

- *become a critical reader*: there are many reasons why you might need to revise and rewrite a draft section of your work. Your word count might be too high or low, your argument may lack clarity, a section might no longer fit your overall plan or you might have developed a more sophisticated approach to an area once you have carried out more research. All these reasons are positive: you can improve your writing style, altering your word count can enhance your argument and the clarity of your evidence and revising a section to incorporate it more effectively into your plan will strengthen your work as a whole. In addition, becoming a critical reader of your own work is pleasurable for its own sake. You will know, as you work through a section, polishing your style and focusing your evidence, that you are making positive changes and you can feel your work improving as you progress.
- *bring your work to life*: if you are focusing upon your style of writing, the easiest way to discover whether you sound too brusque, rambling or pompous is simply to read a section of your work aloud to yourself, over-

dramatising every pause and placing exaggerated emphasis on your phrasing and style. This can feel odd when you first try it, but it is a fail-safe way of becoming a critical reader of your own work and it is the only truly reliable way of 'tone checking' your work, making sure that you have adopted the tone you intended to use. When we read we cannot help but read what we meant to write rather than what we actually did write; by reading your writing aloud problems that would otherwise remain hidden will suddenly spring to life and become blindingly obvious. Once you have completed this exercise on several sections of your work, you can achieve the same effect by reading your work 'aloud' in your head, without needing to actually hear the words.

* *ensure that you are in the right frame of mind*: although revising drafts of your work can be enjoyable, it is always tiring and often more demanding than the original writing, so make sure that you only ever attempt it when you are well rested, not likely to be distracted and feel really positive about what you are attempting to achieve.

* *work from your plan*: if, when you are rewriting, you work solely from your original draft, you risk repeating your initial mistakes. It is better to reduce your word count by taking out paragraphs, altering sections and trimming your style, and then going back to your plan to see whether anything else needs to be included. The same principle applies if you feel that you are losing control of your writing style as you progress. The natural tendency when this happens is simply to keep on writing in the hope that it will correct itself. It probably will, but by that time you may have used several hundred unnecessary words. If you feel this happening to you, stop writing, take a break and then go back to your plan and work from there.

* *get as much help as you can*: draft sections are the best basis for getting targeted help for what you are trying to achieve. However much general advice you receive in supervisions, it is only by producing a draft chapter or section that you can focus on specific problem areas, discuss in minute detail the way in which an argument is progressing or how the entire shape of your project will develop. You need not restrict this valuable input to your supervisions: enlist the help of friends and your study partners or seminar colleagues once you have written a first draft. You will have to be selective: you do not want to bore everyone around you or receive so much advice that it becomes counterproductive, nor do you want to have to reciprocate too many favours once the pressure is on, but some feedback is useful, as long as you retain control of the overall shape of the project.

▶ Creating a bibliography

There are several styles of bibliography from which you can choose and various ways in which you can collate bibliographic material to include within yours. If you are a science or technology postgraduate, you may be producing a list of references rather than a standard bibliography, but there are general guidelines for both that will make what can be a difficult and time-consuming process far more manageable:

*   *begin early*: creating a bibliography is only a nightmare if you leave it until the last minute. When you have completed each section of your dissertation, research report or thesis, go back over your footnotes and write up the bibliography for those footnotes. Although at this stage you might not have decided upon the divisions within your bibliography (primary and secondary texts, for example), you will at least have everything in place when you come to compile the final version.
*   *never miss a reference*: when you update your reading notebooks, never assume that you will remember the full title of a book or article or that you will have plenty of time later to go back and insert the complete details: you will not. Instead, whenever you get tired of your research or run out of useful tasks for the day, spend the spare time updating your reading notebooks. The one reference you do not bother to include is, you can guarantee, the one book that will be lost in the bindery for six months just at the point when you want to check a page number, obscure reference or the full publication details. Remember that these details will be included in your bibliography exactly as they appear in the book, not just as they are listed in a library catalogue: you must use the book itself as your reference, which means noting down the details as you work and including them in your bibliography as you go along.
*   *be consistent*: you do have options about the structure of your bibliography and the referencing system that you choose to use within the text of your work, but you must decide at the outset which system you are using and stick to it. If you are inconsistent, it may not matter much to you but it will stick out like a sore thumb to the examiners.
*   *consider advanced software*: there is software available to aid you in the production of a bibliography and your department might have access to it and provide courses on its use, but nothing will replace a consistent and methodical approach to collating the material as it becomes available to you.
*   *checking takes time*: checking a bibliography is, without doubt, the most boring task that any postgraduate will face. There is no way to make it any less boring, but you can make it bearable in two ways. Firstly, make sure that you have left yourself enough time to check and recheck it thor-

oughly: it always takes longer than you would expect. Secondly, try to allocate specific time slots for this checking. It can be difficult to check a bibliography effectively if you have already spent an hour or so checking the main body of your text: your checking will be far more productive if you allocate an hour later in the day to checking the bibliography alone.

▶ Style

You will already have developed your own style of writing and be capable of adapting your writing to suit your readership, but developing a formal, academic writing style can be quite a challenge, particularly if your experience is limited. If you believe that you might have serious difficulties in this area, there are study skills guides that can help you, but there are ways in which you can help yourself by considering some key aspects of an academic writing style:

* *be concise*: effective written English tends to be concise, clear and to the point, yet when we are under pressure we tend to overreach ourselves, using four words when one would suffice or talking around a point about which we feel uncertain rather than simply stating it. This is not a problem you can always eradicate as you type: if you try too hard you might impede the logical flow of the argument you are making. You can learn to avoid using overly long phrases that often mean nothing ('in point of fact', 'to be fair', 'at this moment in time'), but beyond this you will pick up on wordiness when you make a first check through your work. If you are over your word count, make your first challenge that of reducing your word count by being less wordy; only then should you move on to removing or adapting the contents.

* *use a formal register*: it is difficult to know whether you are using a suitably formal style until you consciously examine your writing in comparison to the writing used in academic journals or textbooks. If you feel that your writing is less formal than you would like, there are some writing techniques that you can check first, before undertaking more substantial work on your style. Do you contract your words (*'don't'* for 'do not', *'we've'* for 'we have' and so on)? You will rarely see this in academic writing, so be aware of it as a potential problem. Do you use rhetorical questions more than is wise? These questions, that you ask and then answer for the reader, are a useful way of catching the reader's attention, but if they are used too often they can become wearing and make your style too informal. Do you tend to use spoken rather than written language? One feature of spoken language that can creep into written

English is the use of connecting words that are redundant ('*So*, it looks as if the evidence is questionable in this area', 'The hypothesis is, *you see*, rather weakened by the evidence', '*All in all*, more work needs to be done in this subject'). The most problematic issue for many postgraduates when they are trying to develop a formal register is the use of 'me' and 'I' in their writing. You will need to discuss this with your supervisor, as it is not always a problem, but a good general rule would be to introduce this way of writing in the introduction ('my research', 'I have endeavoured') and the conclusion ('I have found', 'My conclusions are . . .'), if you find it necessary, but try to avoid it in the main bulk of the text. There are, of course, many more aspects of style you might like to consider, but if you follow the suggestions here you will avoid the worst of the problems; and if this section has left you wondering what on earth it is all about, you might choose to study the subject in more depth.

- *develop your style*: even a discussion of style as brief as this can leave you feeling, wrongly, that your style is underdeveloped and you are going to have to learn a whole new way of writing. This is not the case: you may have to work on some areas of your written language, but your style is your own, unique to you and something to be cherished and developed rather than discarded, so try not to allow yourself to feel inadequate. If you have to make some improvements, that is all they will be, improvements, not a wholesale abandonment of your style of writing.

- *mastering grammar*: you will have a grasp of the basics of English grammar, but there are niceties of grammar that you could master once you begin to write at this level. If, for example, you are not sure how to use a semi-colon, where to place a square bracket or how to indicate a subordinate clause in a sentence, you might like to work on your grammar, not because your dissertation or thesis is necessarily going to be unimpressive if you do not, but because written language has now become one of your principal academic tools, and the more you know, the easier it will be to express yourself in a persuasive and commanding way.

- *pay attention to sentence and paragraph length*: we all use sentences and paragraphs with very little thought: they are the building blocks of our expression. It is unlikely that you will have major problems with them, but if you feel that your writing tends to be rambling, check the sentence length: if most of your sentences exceed 20 words or so, you could try including some shorter sentences. Alternatively, if your writing seems too brusque or note-like, you might find that most of your sentences are shorter than 12 words or so in length, and you could improve your writing by including some longer sentences. As with much else in writing, variety is the key to holding the reader's interest and presenting an engaging argument. Paragraphs are designed to show the division of ideas within a text and allow the reader the chance to 'escape' from the text at designated points, to think about what has been written so far. With this in mind, you will want to begin each new area of discussion with a new paragraph, making it clear to the reader that you are moving on; you will then use as many paragraphs as it takes to complete your discussion, but you will always conclude a paragraph once you have completed that discussion, rather than leading the reader into your next train of thought without the chance to take a break.

- *avoid jargon, colloquialisms, imprecision and clichés*: you will not always be able to think of the perfect word at just the right time: nobody can. However, if you use jargon or a cliché whilst you think of the right word or phrase, or you have to be imprecise and use six words when you feel sure that one word would suffice if only you could think of it, make this clear in your writing. You will not want to interrupt your thoughts by spending too long thinking about it, so make a mark that you will recognise (for example, ###) and when you return to those points as you read through the work, you will find that the correct word or phrase will probably come to you instantly. Once you have revised the work, it is easy to use the 'edit' and 'find' functions on your computer to hunt out any of your symbols (###) that have been left behind in the text by mistake. The edit/find function is also useful when you want to weed out quirky expressions that you have trouble avoiding. If you suspect that you are repeating a phrase too often ('it is often the case that' or 'in my judgement', for example), you can make a note of them, write without hindrance and then check at the end of your writing for the day how often they have been used. You can then replace or delete them without difficultly.

- *remain logical by going back to your plan*: if you are unsure of where your writing is leading, your argument is becoming weak or your style confused, return to your plan to try to relocate yourself within the text. If you just read through your writing, you might have difficulty in distancing yourself from it enough to take control, whereas a brief check back to your plan will refocus your thoughts and give you the confidence to return to your writing in a logical and authoritative way.

- *check for 'dips' in your style*: however careful you are, it is simply not possible to produce the perfect script at the first point of writing. You will check and recheck, revise and adapt, and still you will miss the occasional typing error or peculiarity of expression. If you have a study partner, family or friends who can help, they will eradicate many of these minor errors but there might still be an insidious problem lurking in the text. As we come to the end of a paragraph, we naturally tend to think about how we will open the next paragraph. As we approach the conclusion of a section, we are either thinking with relief of what we might do next or begining to worry about how this section should fit into the overall plan. Our writing therefore tends to 'dip' two-thirds or three-quarters of the way through a lengthy paragraph, section or chapter. When you are checking through your work for the umpteenth time and are perhaps too familiar with it, it is not necessarily productive simply to plough through it all again in the hope that mistakes will leap out of the page at you. Instead, target your final checking on the sentences or paragraphs in this location: there will be more errors to spot here and you are more likely to see them if you take this approach.

- *always remain aware of your readership*: as you write up your research, you will probably have a reader in your mind's eye, perhaps your supervisor or study partner, or your ideal reader if you hope to publish your work. When you come to check through your text in its final stages, you will have to dispense with this reader and remember that your work will be read widely, by internal and external examiners and, perhaps, by a wider reading public. All your diagrams and tables will have to be clearly labelled, all your terms must be explained and you will have to make your meaning crystal clear for those readers who have not discussed the work with you in advance of their reading. This is not difficult, but it is essential if you are to persuade your readers of your argument and keep them interested and enthusiastic for the duration of your work.

Questions of style and the challenges of grammar and punctuation will be resolved, for the most part, as your course progresses. You will become adept at managing a word count, skilled in creating a bibliography and confident about your ability to write up an extensive piece of research in a way that does credit to your intellect and academic rigour. The guidelines offered in this chapter will ensure that you avoid disasters, and the advice offered in the previous chapters will help you to manage your postgraduate course in such a way that it becomes not only a challenge but also a pleasure. Ultimately, you will have produced an impressive piece of independent research and you will have gained an enviable qualification: you will be ready to progress onto the next stage of your career.

Spot guide

The key points to remember from this chapter:

- discuss the timing of your writing up with your supervisor
- leave enough time in your personalised timetable to produce a detailed plan
- decide which planning methods work best for you
- vary your planning methods for differing sections of your plan
- include your word count and timing in each section of your final plan
- check back to your research sheets and reading and research notebooks before you finalise your plan
- try not to worry too much about word counts until you are sure you have a problem
- use drafts and rewrites to sharpen your arguments and polish your style
- become a critical reader of your written output
- get help from as many sources as possible
- work on your style, one step at a time
- be clear about practicalities, such as bindery deadlines and how long your supporters will require to check through your work
- never leave your bibliography until the last minute: produce it as you write and note down every reference as you use it

11 Moving on from your Postgraduate Course

Troubleshooting guide

Use this chapter for help in the following areas:

- if you have not yet developed a career strategy
- if you are unsure of the commerical value of some of your academic activities
- if you are not sure how to find out about the careers available to you
- if you have little experience in approaching the job market
- if you are anxious about making direct contact with potential employers
- if you do not have an effective or up-to-date curriculum vitae (CV)
- if you need help in producing a research proposal
- if you are unsure about the difference between a commerical and an academic CV

You have successfully completed your course and you are now facing the next challenge: breaking into a career. This transition will be easier if you have followed the advice in earlier chapters: you will already have considered your academic and career options and have a skills portfolio. Now there is more work to do.

▶ Focusing on the future

In some ways this is a difficult time to consider your future, in that you will feel relief that your course is over, perhaps tinged with sadness that a satisfying phase of your life is finishing, whilst being elated that you have finally achieved your desired result. Thinking about your career may be the last

170

thing on your mind at the moment. On the other hand, your recent experience, your desirability from an employer's point of view and your will to succeed will all be fresh in your mind.

You need some space, some time to think things over, and this will have such an impact upon your future that it is important to take some time off if you possibly can: even a week with nothing else to do will help to boost your energy and clarify your thoughts. You may not change your mind about your overall plans, but you will be in a better position to put them into practice. As most postgraduates get a new job (or return to their existing career, often at a higher level) once they have completed their courses, the main focus of this chapter will be on this area. However, much of the advice will be relevant if you are applying for a further course and there will be a section dedicated to applying for academic courses and funding.

Once you have recharged your mental batteries, you can begin to create a 'career file'; this will form the basis of your CV and application forms. This might look a little like your reading and research notebooks, with ideas about your skills and experience jotted down as they occur to you, or you might type up each section so that you have the details on disk ready to incorporate into a CV or interview preparation sheet. There are several areas of your time at university that might be included in your career file.

Paid work

The advantage of creating a career file at this stage is that you will not forget the minor details of a job: these are often attractive from the point of view of a prospective employer even if the job itself was not very impressive to you. It may be, for example, that you spent six weeks working behind the bar of your local pub, but you might also have organised the local pub quiz night for charity. This may have been only a minor part of your overall job, but it allows you to demonstrate to an employer that you have begun to develop organisational skills, experience in PR and leadership qualities. This will help to counteract any view an employer might have about postgraduates spending their time buried in libraries, rarely seeing the light of day or interacting with other people.

Career placements

These schemes are obviously a good chance to develop your work-related skills. If you have undertaken a vocational course, they may have formed the core of your university experience. It is a good idea to get a copy of the report made on you by the employer, if this is possible. The report given to your university may be confidential but this does not prevent you from asking directly for a reference. Employers often use career placements as easy talking points at interview, so whether you found your placement a pleasure or a pain, make sure that, as soon as possible after the event, you write down a succinct account of what you have achieved and how it related to your course. No employer is going to want to hear a blow by blow account of every day that you spent on placement, but if you make notes you can rehearse your account before your interview, remembering to stress the good points, the positive aspects of the placement and the skills you acquired in the process.

Joint projects

It is highly unlikely that you will have undertaken the whole of your postgraduate course in isolation. At the very least you will have been part of a team in a seminar situation and Chapter 8 will have helped you to identify other teams within which you have worked. It is a common misconception that employers are just looking for the most qualified person for a job. In fact, any organisation, commercial or otherwise, is simply an extended team, and employers are looking to employ someone who will fit into that team. They can always train you: that is usually far cheaper than having to readvertise the position and go through the whole selection process again because they have employed someone who cannot work as a constructive member of their team.

Presentations

You will have given presentations in some capacity as a postgraduate and it is important that your potential employer knows that you have undertaken this task. There is another advantage to having given presentations as a postgraduate. One of the questions often asked at interview is how you have overcome any difficulties in the past. If you are able to explain how you faced up to and overcame a problem with a presentation, you can answer the question in a way that is both honest and positive.

Your extended research project

Although this book has focused on the means by which you produce a dissertation, thesis or research report, you now have to consider those aspects of the experience that will impress an employer and include them in your career file. You will be able to show, for example, that you can work under pressure, can think independently about ideas and concepts and have a creative flair. You will also be able to prove that you have excellent time management skills. You might know that you produced much of your work at the last minute in a flat spin, but the employer does not know that, and the fact that you did achieve the necessary result within a stipulated time period is all that matters now. When an employer asks about your research at interview, you need not confuse the issue with a detailed account of the specialist aspects of your research if this is not directly relevant to the job. The employer is seeking to identify those points that will sell you as an employee, so prepare your answer in advance, finding ways in which you can describe your research so that anyone can understand what you have done, taking the opportunity to stress the skills you acquired in the process. You do not have to be too strait-laced about this: it is perfectly acceptable to smile about any difficulties you encountered, but make sure that your account is upbeat and positive.

▶ Breaking into the career market

It is an often publicised fact that the vast majority of vacancies are not advertised: the figure is sometimes put as high as 80 per cent. This leaves you with a dilemma: you know that the jobs are out there somewhere, you suspect there are fewer opportunities available to you as a postgraduate because you are now much choosier about your career and you are not sure exactly which job you want or how to get it. The first thing to do is to carry out some research. You might already have some options in place from your networking and your course may have been designed to prepare its students for a particular career area. Even if this is the case, carry out some careers research and think as widely as you can before committing yourself. Your university's Careers Advisory Service is not just for undergraduates: they will be able to work through the possibilities with you, administering personality and aptitude tests to help you to narrow down the options. You can adopt a two-stage approach to the task by getting a job to raise some cash whilst you look for the perfect career opening; the suggestions here will apply equally to both stages.

Once you have decided upon an area, or more probably several areas, that interest you, you are still left with the problem of succeeding in the job market. There are several ways in which you can tackle this, and using a combination of all these approaches will give you the best chance of success.

Careers fairs
Careers fairs can be crowded out by eager undergraduates, but this does not prevent you from taking a look at what is on offer. Remember that you are making judgements about the organisations that are at the fair as well as allowing them to assess you as a potential employee. Make sure that you gather as much information as you can in this relatively informal setting, but keep an eye on the people who are there to represent each organisation. If

they seem negative, rather too pushy for your liking or, as can sometimes happen, they just look downright miserable, take this as a reflection of the organisation for which they are working. If you like the look of the organisation, but the representatives have no clear idea about postgraduate options, make sure you do your own research by contacting the organisation directly as part of your careers search.

Departmental information

Your supervisor will be your starting point here, but there is only so much that can be achieved by networking with just one person, so do not rely solely on this contact. Departments sometimes hold detailed information about the career destinations of past postgraduates and this can be an easy way of beginning your research. It may be possible for you to make contact directly with postgraduates who have successfully entered a career area in which you have an interest. As with so much else, your departmental secretary will be able to point you in the right direction.

Newspapers

Newspapers are an obvious place to begin your job hunt, but be as creative as you can in your searching and remember that whilst organisations might be recruiting new graduates, this does not mean that they have no vacancies suitable for postgraduates. If, for example, you notice that a particular organisation is placing several adverts for different positions, you can be reasonably sure that they are running a recruitment drive and it will be worth your while to contact them in case they are extending their recruitment to an area that is of interest to you. Specialist journals in your field will carry advertisements for vacancies, particularly if you are looking for work in the social sciences, and you will know the best place to look for work that will interest you. Again, do not just take the information at face value: if an organisation looks interesting, give them a call.

The Internet

The Internet is an increasingly accessible and popular source of information about careers and job vacancies and it is one to which you will turn early on in your search. Make sure you are targeted in your approach or you might waste hours looking at sites that are of only marginal use to you, or simply logging on to the sites that are run by job agencies, when a direct approach to employers might be more productive. If you find an organisation that interests you, use the Internet to find out as much as you can about the organisation and then contact them directly.

Job agencies

There are many useful job agencies, but many more will be useless to you, either because they do not specialise in your field of interest or they are over-loaded with candidates and short of vacancies to offer them. Be selective: find out which are the best agencies to contact and then take control of the situation. If they want to produce a CV for you, make sure that you have the final say on its content and presentation. If they want to send you for an interview, make absolutely certain that you know where they are sending you and that the job is at a level that reflects your postgraduate status.

Networking

Networking is an effective way to carry out your career search, but it will take some work. You will already have some networks in place and a full email address book of contacts who might be useful to you, although you will obviously want to approach the task with some caution: a blanket request for help might hinder your efforts rather than helping them. It is a good idea to create a career network before you complete your course: this consists of a group of colleagues who can remain in contact via email in order to pass on information about jobs and career opportunities. You may have seen these people regularly at university, but once you leave you can lose contact with surprising ease. If you set up this fairly formal means of networking whilst you are all still together, you will give yourself the best chance of working as an effective networking group in the future; these groups can last for years, as you all progress into new areas of your careers.

Direct contact

Direct contact is the most challenging, but also the most effective way to get into a career. By contacting organisations direct you will be getting behind the advertised job market into what is often referred to as the 'hidden job market', where jobs vacancies are filled by word of mouth rather than a formal recruitment procedure. You might be making 'warm calls', that is, contacting an employer who you met at a conference or as a result of a career or research placement, or 'cold calls', where you will be approaching an organisation without any knowledge of whether it is recruiting or not. Making direct contact is an efficient use of your time and will be necessary even if you are responding to an advert: in this case, you will need to know whether the vacancy still exists (this can save you hours of wasted time), whether you can fill their requirements and whether the organisation is one that suits you. There are techniques to this approach that you will need to master:

- Do the research: if you have heard of an organisation that interests you, find out as much as you can about it, perhaps through a website or by getting hold of a company brochure.

- Prepare your paperwork in advance: before you telephone, have your CV in front of you, with a list of questions you want to ask and a pen and paper ready to take notes. Be ready for your enquiry to turn into an informal telephone interview. If you realise that there are new questions you can ask in future calls, add them to your list as you go along. You will probably find that, by the end of the first three calls, your 'script' is twice as long as it was at the outset.

- Have a series of telephone calls arranged before you begin: make a list of a dozen organisations that appeal to you and then brace yourself to make all the calls in one day.

- Do not be disappointed if you cannot get through to the human resources department on your first try: receptionists can be an invaluable source of information not readily available elsewhere, so keep them talking about the organisation if you can. You can always call back another time if you cannot get through to the right department on your first attempt.

- Begin with your least favoured option and work up. You might find that on your first call your mouth goes dry and you forget what you wanted to say. It will not matter if this call is a disaster: you have plenty more options in front of you. You will be amazed at how quickly you become adept at this exercise. I have seen postgraduates who were quivering wrecks on the first call become dynamic salespeople by the third.

- If you suspect that the first call is going to be a nightmare, when you might forget what you wanted to say or just dry up altogether, dial 141 (so that your number cannot be traced) before you make the call and, if it all goes wrong, just put the telephone down. They will never know who was calling them and you can try again later when you become more expert.

- Be ready to enjoy yourself. Although this exercise can be a terrifying prospect, comfort yourself with the fact that it is probably the best way to get a job and you will find that, with practice, it can be a satisfying and enjoyable process.

- Avoid the temptation to be negative. If an organisation has no vacancies for postgraduates at the moment, this does not mean that it will not have any jobs on offer next week. If you can get a conversation going, and arrange to send your CV, someone can get back to you when an opportunity arises: this really does happen. It is expensive for an organisation to recruit new staff: if your details are on file it is more cost-effective for it to come back to you direct when a vacancy arises. If you want to make yourself even more visible, and it seems appropriate, ask to visit its premises so as to learn more about how it operates. This will give you the chance to have an informal chat in advance of any positions becoming vacant.

* See this as a fact-finding mission. This exercise is as much about you exploring what an organisation has to offer as it is about you being vetted by it. If the receptionist is rude and the manager is unhelpful and unsure about what is on offer, you might decide that you are not interested in it, which will save you the trouble of applying to it when it does advertise vacancies.

You have two challenges ahead of you as you target your new career. You are trying to find out exactly where you want to be in the future and researching all the possible leads, but you are doing this whilst still trying to get used to the 'new you', the successful postgraduate who has so much more to offer an employer. By targeting the career market directly, doing your research and making the telephone calls, you will be tackling both these areas. As you carry out your career research, you will get a better idea of where to go and as you call organisations, you will feel increasingly confirmed in your new status.

▶ Creating a CV

Getting into the right job often seems to involve mountains of paperwork. You will need to be organised before you begin. Keep a file on each organisation you have approached, so that you can refer back to the notes you made during the telephone call, the application form you filled in and the CV you sent. Keeping your records up to date need not be a chore: in reality, you will find it reassuring as it imposes some structure on what can be a relatively unstructured period of your life. When you become anxious about your chances of getting a job, you can look into your files and remind yourself that you are doing everything you can do towards that end, which is a comfort if things seem to be moving too slowly.

Although you are likely to be asked to complete an application form at some stage of the recruitment process, this is not necessarily the principal document in your career search. If you succeed in a telephone call, you will probably be asked to send your CV to the organisation. In some cases, successful candidates are asked to complete an application form only after they have been interviewed, just to satisfy the protocol of the organisation concerned. Your CV is going to be vital to you.

You will already have some idea of what to include in your CV from your career file, but before you begin to write anything down, you need to take a step back and consider what you want your CV to do for you. You are trying to sell yourself to an employer and, like any successful marketing strategy, you need to know as much as you can about the sales situation before you begin. There are three main points to bear in mind:

1. *Know who are.* That is, know who you are from the point of view of employment. What are you selling? What are your unique selling points? How do your selling points differ now that you have completed your postgraduate course? Once you have completed your CV, pin it up somewhere where you can see it every day. This will boost your confidence and remind you of the professional image you are projecting.
2. *Know where you want to be.* Even if you are applying for a vacancy that has been advertised, you will not have enough information from an advert to make the best sales pitch. You will need to make a telephone call to find out more about the vacancy and the organisation.
3. *Know what they want.* You can usually get hold of a copy of a full job description and person specification if you contact the organisation, which will give you essential clues about how to target your CV and application form. If you check its website or get a copy of its company brochure or marketing material, you can learn about the culture of the organisation and work out what sort of person it is likely to employ.

At every stage in this process of learning about your prospective employer, remember that you are free to pull out. You have not even begun to write your CV or fill out an application form, so if your instinct is telling you that this is not the right company for you, trust to it and move ahead with your next prospect.

If the organisation is still one to which you want to apply once you have done the initial research, you will begin to prepare your CV. Remember that your CV is your sales pitch, so you have to make each word count. Although you will work within the most effective format for you, the CV outlined below is one that tends to work well for postgraduates. I have taken for this example a candidate who has successfully completed a postgraduate diploma in marketing and is applying for a job as a corporate client manager with a large marketing firm.

Curriculum Vitae
Carole Anne Foster

65 Walkers Close, Taunton, Somerset, TN14 7PQ
Tel: (0143) 221 5690; mobile: (07234) 101 6787
email: cafoster@aol.com

A marketing postgraduate with recent professional experience and a keen commerical awareness. A team player with excellent communication skills and a flexible and enthusiastic approach to each new challenge.

Relevant skills and experience

Marketing: During my postgraduate course I spent a six-week career placement with a PR firm, gaining a valuable insight into the field of marketing.

Communication: I have experience of dealing with clients by telephone, letter and in person. As a member of my university debating society, I was given the opportunity to develop a range of communication skills.

Teamwork: I have worked as a member of several successful teams giving group presentations, arranging conferences and undertaking research projects.

Organisation: I am a highly organised individual and this was vital to the successful completion of my dissertation, which was delivered on time and to the specified requirements and for which I gained a distinction.

Information technology: I have undertaken courses in Office 2000, Front Page and PowerPoint. I am keen to continue to develop my IT skills in the workplace.

Education

2002–2003: Postgraduate Diploma in Marketing, specialising in the impact of European legislation upon current marketing trends in the UK.

Continued

1999–2002: Honours Degree (2:1) in English with modules also successfully completed in History and Sociology. My dissertation, entitled 'Communication in the Modern Workplace', formed an important part of my degree course.

1997–1999: A levels gained in English (A), History (A) and Law (C); AS levels gained in English, History, Law and Sociology; GCSEs gained in ten subjects, including English, Mathematics, ICT, French and German

Professional development

Courses undertaken in Office 2000, Front Page and PowerPoint. I have a working knowledge of a variety of design packages and some experience of accounting software.

As part of my career placement with Interscan PR and Marketing, I carried out a feasibility study on the potential for European involvement in a major PR initiative. I also attended a course entitled 'The Way Ahead: European Directives within Marketing.'

Career history

July 2003 to present: Since the successful completion of my postgraduate course, I have worked on a voluntary basis for a major charity. My role has included:

- arranging public information events
- providing administrative support for a team of six
- organising fund-raising activities.

November to December 2002: Six-week career placement with Interscan, a PR and marketing firm concerned with the launch of IT packages and the provision of software support. My role included:

- providing support for my corporate client manager at all stages of account development
- arranging marketing meetings for up to 20 members of staff
- undertaking statistical analysis of market research data.

Additional information

I am a member of the Institute of Marketing.
I am currently attending a course in Business and Conversational French.
I hold a first aid certificate.

I am physically fit and have a current driving licence.

My interests include reading (I particularly enjoy political biographies), sport and cinema (I am a member of my local film appreciation society).

References are available on request

As you can see, this CV makes the most of all aspects of our student's postgraduate experience. It foregrounds her commerical experience and highlights her team skills, presentation abilities and academic success. She has targeted her CV to this particular job and provided plenty of useful starting points for discussion at interview. She will have left out some information she thinks is less relevant to this job, but will have kept it on file ready for use at interview or in further CVs.

▶ An academic career

If you are considering enrolling on a further course, you will be able to refer back to the guidance offered in Chapters 1 and 2, but there are two tasks you will need to approach now. You might have to produce a research proposal, particularly if you are applying for funding, and you will have to produce an academic CV. If you are hoping to enter an academic career at this stage, you will be bringing into play all your networking options, as well as working through the advice offered in this chapter.

Research proposals differ vastly from one institution and funding body to another and there is no substitute for carrying out research and discovering exactly what is required of you. Beyond this, contact your supervisor rather than assuming that, now you have successfully completed your course, the relationship is at an end. Your proposal might be brief, confined to the pages of a form similar to a job application, or it might be a more extended piece of work, designed to test the feasibility of your proposed project. There are books available to help you in this process, but there are some guidelines that are worth keeping in mind, regardless of the form that your research proposal takes.

Do:
• Ensure that you have the timing right: know exactly when each stage of your application is due to be completed.
• Fill out every form that is sent to you, complete and in the format required.

- Leave yourself more time than you ever thought possible to fill out the forms, collect references and so on.
- Inform referees and your potential supervisor of your intentions and each step you take.
- Give a copy of the completed forms to each of your referees and make sure that they are aware of the time frame within which you are working.
- Network as widely as you can: you might find useful funding opportunities in the least expected places.
- Check (on the Internet and elsewhere) the details of the funding body to which you are applying: you might discover that it favours certain types of project or has a 'frequently asked questions' (FAQs) section on its website.
- Make sure that you are aware of, and mention, every current publication which might have a bearing on your research.
- Demonstrate originality in your proposal: how will your work add to the sum of knowledge in your area?

Do not:
- Forget to have a backup plan: what will you do if your application is unsuccessful?
- Ignore any of the options available to you, however remote they seem at first glance.
- Assume that everyone involved in your application is as enthusiastic, or as efficient, as you are.
- Just see the application process as a form-filling exercise: it is a chance to test how viable your proposed research is when it is fleshed out.
- Assume that the panel making a decision on your proposal or application is as informed as you are: use accessible language and be clear about what you intend to achieve.
- See the process as a 'one-off': keep your notes on file for future use.
- Be hesitant about contacting the funding body if you are unsure about any instructions you have been given.
- Ignore the help on offer from your department and Careers Advisory Service.
- Worry too much about your proposal once it has been submitted: get on with other projects whilst you await a decision.
- Expect a swift response: it will be some time before you discover whether you have been successful.

Once you have written your research proposal, you will need to turn to your CV. An academic CV differs from a commerical or professional CV in that it aims to highlight your academic achievements and potential. As with any

CV, you will target each version of your CV to the academic career move or course for which you are applying, but the example CV given here uses a format that will work well in most academic situations. I have taken for this example a postgraduate who has completed an MA in History and is putting forward a proposal for a three-year doctorate in his specialist area, backed up by this CV.

Curriculum Vitae
Terence Seddon

21 Drovers Place, Gloucester, GL5 6TB
Tel: (0968) 555 9102; mobile: (07451) 445 7878
email: tjseddon@aol.com

Academic record

2002–2003: MA (Distinction) from Warwick University: Family and Society in Early Modern London
This involved the study of a wide variety of Early Modern texts, including treatise on childbirth, medical manuals and family papers, as well as literary works, both within and without the established literary canon. I also undertook extensive research within the archival resources in several major libraries. The aim of the course was to foster an understanding of the effect of demographic trends upon family life in Early Modern London, in addition to encouraging students to consider how these trends might impact upon society in other regions. I was able to develop a historical, cultural and literary approach to a multidisciplinary area of research. I gained distinction in all my coursework and in my final dissertation, which was entitled 'Rites of passage: a case study of births, marriages and deaths within six families in the parish of Blackheath, 1650–1700.'

1999–2002: BA (Hons) First Class in History from Newcastle University
My course covered a wide range of historical periods and methodologies. I specialised in Early Modern History and successfully completed a dissertation entitled 'Demographic trends in relation to trade statistics in Suffolk, 1650–1680.' I also undertook optional courses that proved valuable during my MA:

Continued

- mastering statistics: introductory and intermediate courses undertaken
- mathematical modelling with reference to demographic trends
- predicting our future by understanding our past
- research techniques in History
- utilising advanced methodologies.

Publications and conferences

I am currently awaiting publication of an article in the journal *History Now*, entitled 'Blackheath in transition: case studies in demographic anomalies, 1660–1675.' I also have three papers ready for publication.

I have given papers at conferences and seminars at the Universities of Newcastle, Reading, Leeds and Cambridge. Two of these papers are due to be included in university publications.

I have led undergraduate seminars within the Departments of History and Sociology at Warwick University.

During my postgraduate course I became involved in a research development group whose aim was to disseminate research and publication information amongst postgraduates. I have also chaired meetings of my local history society.

I have been a tour guide for historical tours of London during university vacations.

Research aims

My aim during the research outlined in my proposal would be to investigate the development of family life within society in the Early Modern period with reference to demographic trends and cultural rites of passage. Through publication and conference papers I hope to encourage debate about the relative importance of anecdotal evidence, court reports and statistical data to the study of family life in this period. In addition, I hope to be able to continue to develop my theories as to the relevance of rites of passage to the experience of family life and explore the impact that demographic changes have had upon these rites, family life and wider society as a whole.

You will notice that this CV differs markedly from the professional CV given earlier. Our postgraduate has not highlighted any paid work he has done, although he has mentioned in passing some of his work experience that might be relevant to his current proposal. What he is aiming to show here is potential: not only the potential of his proposed research, but also his potential as an academic.

▶ Achieving success

Whichever route you hope to take once you have completed your course, you will have some work to do, but this can in itself be pleasurable and constructive. If you are making a research proposal, you will focus upon your excellent academic achievements and your skills as a researcher. If you are researching the career market, you will be reminding yourself at all times that you are a postgraduate, possessed of a respected qualification that will gain you access to the ideal career for you. It might take some time, it will certainly take some effort, but it will be worth it. In the years to come you will be able to look back at your postgraduate course as not only a turning point in your life, but also one of the most satisfying periods of your career. You will have learnt a lot about your subject, but discovered even more about yourself and the person you have become. Good luck!

Spot guide

The key points to remember from this chapter:

- everything you have done whilst at university will be useful to you as you progress
- make a career file, in which you can gather information about your skills and achievements as you go along
- use as many sources of information as possible in your search for a career break or research option
- create a careers network with your fellow postgraduates
- making direct contact with organisations is the most effective way to move ahead in your career
- see your CV as your main sales pitch and work on it as you progress, targeting it to each new opportunity
- use your Careers Advisory Service and supervisor to the full
- try to impose some structure on your career search: this will help to keep you motivated

Index

A/B
articulating your ideas, 47–50
assessment of prior learning, 3
bibliography, 164–5

C
career file, 171–3
career search, 173–7
combined courses, 5
conference papers, 140–3
conferences, academic, 30–2
connections in your research,
    86–7
continuous assessment, 19–20
course accreditation, 10–11
coursework, 18–19
curriculum vitae, 177–81, 182–5

D
department/university teams, 126
discussion groups, 32–3, 87
distance and open learning courses,
    5–6
drafts and rewrites, 162–3

E
e-learning, 34–6
established courses, 14–15
examination workshops, 16
examinations, 16–18, 107–8
extending your course, 100–1

F
failing, 114–15
financial planning, 14, 105–6
flexibility in your course, 12–13

I
independent research, 20–1
Internet and catalogue connections,
    88
isolation, 108–10

L
learning outcomes, 11–12
lectures, 27–8, 82–4
libraries and resource centres, 101–3

M/N/O
missing a seminar or lecture, 103–4
note-taking, 82–4
occasional teams, 127

P
personalised timetable, 93–7
placements, 36–8
plagiarism, 84
planning effectively, 58–9, 152–9
presentations, 53–4, 107–8, 125
problem-solving, 54–5
professional development, 2–3
publication, 143–6

Q/R
qualifications to apply for a course,
    9–10
reading productively, 42–6
record-keeping, 85
research courses, 4–5
research presentations, 133–7
research proposals, 181–2
research sheets, 90–2
research-tagging, 85–6

research teams, 124–5
researching a course, 13

S
seminar presentations, 137–40
seminar/class teams, 124
seminars, 25–7, 108
skill development plan, 59–63
skills base assessment, 41–2
social teams, 128–9
study partnerships, 87–8, 130–1
supervision, 20–1
supervisor, choosing a, 65–8
supervisor, communicating with, 73–4
supervisor, working with, 68–77
supervisor/supervisee teams, 126–7
support for your studying, 113–14
support teams, 129–30

T
taught courses, 4
teamwork, 117–23
thinking creatively, 55–8
time management, 92–7, 104–5, 110–11,
    122, 149–52
tiredness, 115–16
tutorials, 33–4

V/W
visiting speakers, 28–30
word count, 159–62
work-based projects, 38–9
work-based courses, 6
work teams, 128
writing skills, 50–3, 165–8